MORE
DANCE IMPROVISATIONS

Justine Reeve,
BA, PGCE, PGDip

HUMAN KINETICS

Library of Congress Cataloging-in-Publication Data

Names: Reeve, Justine, author.
Title: More dance improvisations / Justine Reeve, BA, PGCE, PGDip.
Description: First edition. | Champaign, IL : Human Kinetics, [2024]
Identifiers: LCCN 2023007887 (print) | LCCN 2023007888 (ebook) | ISBN 9781718222427 (print) | ISBN 9781718222434 (epub) | ISBN 9781718222441 (pdf)
Subjects: LCSH: Improvisation in dance.
Classification: LCC GV1781.2 .R443 2024 (print) | LCC GV1781.2 (ebook) | DDC 792.802/8—dc23/eng/20230512
LC record available at https://lccn.loc.gov/2023007887
LC ebook record available at https://lccn.loc.gov/2023007888

ISBN: 978-1-7182-2242-7 (print)

Copyright © 2024 by Human Kinetics, Inc.

Human Kinetics supports copyright. Copyright fuels scientific and artistic endeavor, encourages authors to create new works, and promotes free speech. Thank you for buying an authorized edition of this work and for complying with copyright laws by not reproducing, scanning, or distributing any part of it in any form without written permission from the publisher. You are supporting authors and allowing Human Kinetics to continue to publish works that increase the knowledge, enhance the performance, and improve the lives of people all over the world.

To report suspected copyright infringement of content published by Human Kinetics, contact us at **permissions@hkusa.com**. To request permission to legally reuse content published by Human Kinetics, please refer to the information at **https://US.HumanKinetics.com/pages/permissions-information**.

The web addresses cited in this text were current as of March 2023, unless otherwise noted.

Acquisitions Editor: Bethany J. Bentley; **Managing Editor:** Anne E. Mrozek; **Permissions Manager:** Laurel Mitchell; **Senior Graphic Designer:** Joe Buck; **Cover Designer:** Keri Evans; **Cover Design Specialist:** Susan Rothermel Allen; **Photograph (cover):** David McHugh; **Photographs (interior):** David McHugh, unless otherwise noted; **Photo Asset Manager:** Laura Fitch; **Photo Production Manager:** Jason Allen; **Production:** Westchester Publishing Services; **Printer:** Color House Graphics, Inc.

Printed in the United States of America

10 9 8 7 6 5 4 3 2 1

The paper in this book is certified under a sustainable forestry program.

Human Kinetics
1607 N. Market Street
Champaign, IL 61820
USA

United States and International
Website: **US.HumanKinetics.com**
Email: info@hkusa.com
Phone: 1-800-747-4457

Canada
Website: **Canada.HumanKinetics.com**
Email: info@hkcanada.com

E9178

CONTENTS

Improvisation Finder   v • Preface   ix
Acknowledgements   xi

1 INTRODUCTION AND HOW TO USE THIS BOOK   1

This chapter explores how to use this book, warming up and safe practice, effective planning, top tips for dance improvisation, planning your workshop, inclusive practice, finding the right music, musicality and phrases.

2 WARM-UP GAMES AND IMPROVISATIONS   15

This chapter explores the concepts of play and spontaneous movement as stimuli for warming up the body and preparing the mind for new experiences. The games and improvisations within will prepare dancers for the creative tasks ahead, improve reaction times and explore key features of movement.

3 SOLO AND DUO IMPROVISATIONS   47

This chapter explores the movement responses dancers can generate on their own and with partners. Through these tasks, they'll discover spontaneous movement answers that will develop, challenge and refine their creative responses, solo or in duos.

4 GROUP IMPROVISATIONS 83

This chapter explores the movement responses dancers can generate in groups. By working with others, they can explore and discover new movement ideas. The tasks within aim to develop, challenge and refine creative responses and the feeling of working as a team that comes with making group decisions in the moment.

5 MOVING BEYOND THE KINAESTHETIC: USING PHYSICAL AND AURAL IMPROVISATION TASKS 115

This chapter explores how starting with elements of physical and aural settings can lead students to create interesting, well-thought-out and purposeful dance. It acts as a taster for being inspired by external stimuli and will hopefully inspire an abundance of future ideas.

6 DEVELOPING IMPROVISATIONS 149

This chapter encourages dancers to use the movements, phrases and sequences created in previous tasks to play with development and structuring to manipulate the movement material. They can also develop ideas using existing material and repertoire. These are only a few suggestions to inspire additional ideas on how to develop movements into dance pieces or works.

Choreographic Tool Kit 181
About the Author 187

IMPROVISATION FINDER

Improvisation name	Page number	Organisational pattern	Approximate duration	Difficulty level
Accumulation	170	Small groups	15-30 min	Moderate
All in the Eyes	52	Partners	5-15 min	Moderate
Applaud the Stars	20	Whole group roaming	5-10 min	Easy
At the Same Time	34	Whole groups	5-10 min	Moderate
Awareness	60	Partners	10-15 min	Moderate/Complex
Background	158	Partners, small groups	15-25 min	Moderate
Battle Lines	88	Small groups, lines	10-20 min	Moderate
Be Original	112	Small groups	10-20 min	Moderate/Complex
Bob the Obstacle	94	Small groups	10-20 min	Easy
Body as Set	92	Small groups	10-20 min	Moderate
Chalk It Up	135	Partners, small groups	10-15 min	Moderate
Coin Creations	176	Partners	15-30 min	Moderate
Connection Perfection	86	Small groups	10-15 min	Complex
Developing Physical Skills	153	Solo	15-30 min	Moderate
Devices Surprises	155	Solo	15-30 min	Moderate
Discussing Dance	178	Small groups	15-30 min	Easy
Disrupt the Air	68	Solo, partners	10-15 min	Moderate
Double Numbers	24	Whole group	5-10 min	Easy
Drawing Whilst Supported	70	Partners	10-20 min	Complex
En Masse	106	Whole group, small groups	5-15 min	Easy
Epic Journey	80	Solo, partners	10-20 min	Easy
Falling and Failing	64	Partners	10-15 min	Moderate
Falling Through Centre	56	Solo	5-15 min	Moderate
Finding the Essence	172	Groups	15-30 min	Moderate/Complex
Find the Phrasing	143	Whole group	10-20 min	Moderate
Flight Path	120	Small groups	15-30 min	Moderate/Complex
Formation Station	166	Small groups	15-30 min	Moderate
Graffiti	110	Small groups	5-20 min	Moderate

(continued) >

Improvisation Finder (continued)

Improvisation name	Page number	Organisational pattern	Approximate duration	Difficulty level
Helping Hands	66	Partners	10-20 min	Moderate/Complex
Into and Back Out	164	Small groups	15-30 min	Moderate
Just the Music	141	Partners	10-20 min	Easy
Layering in Pathways	168	Small groups	15-30 min	Moderate
Lead, Refine, Repeat	96	Small groups	10-15 min	Easy
Lighting Line	74	Solo	10-20 min	Moderate/Complex
Make and Break	104	Small groups	10-20 min	Moderate
Making an Entrance	108	Whole group, small groups	10-20 min	Easy
Make Some Noise	26	Whole group, solo	5-10 min	Easy
Making Maps	54	Partners	5-15 min	Moderate
Moments of Stillness	162	Solo	20-30 min	Moderate
Narrative in Music	147	Solo, partners, small groups	15-30 min	Moderate
Orbit Swing	118	Solo, partners	20-40 min	Complex
Park Bench	137	Whole group	15-30 min	Moderate
People Watching	122	Partners	5-15 min	Easy
Playing Your Part	145	Small groups	10-20 min	Moderate
Pointing Game	18	Whole group roaming, partners	5-10 min	Easy
Practice and Emphasis	160	Solo	15-30 min	Moderate
Quality	38	Whole group roaming	5-15 min	Moderate
Quiet Links	98	Small groups	10-15 min	Easy
Recall, Remember and Move On	58	Partners	10-20 min	Moderate/Complex
Rehearsals	174	Small groups	15-30 min	Moderate
Repetitive Dance	42	Whole group	5-10 min	Easy
Reportage	124	Partners, small groups	5-20 min	Moderate
Rhythm Connection	139	Whole group	10-20 min	Easy
Running to the Middle	44	Whole group, circle	5-10 min	Easy

Improvisation name	Page number	Organisational pattern	Approximate duration	Difficulty level
Sending a Message	40	Whole group, partners	5-10 min	Easy
Setting a Route	134	Whole group	10-20 min	Moderate
Shifting Space	78	Solo, partners	10-15 min	Easy/Moderate
Simple Commands	126	Partners	5-20 min	Moderate
Slow Group	100	Small groups	10-15 min	Easy
Snap	28	Whole group	5-10 min	Easy
Someone's Coming!	36	Whole group	5-10 min	Easy
Space Swapping Duet	62	Partners	10-20 min	Moderate
Struggle	90	Small groups	15-30 min	Complex
Swing Time	30	Whole group	5-15 min	Moderate
Tennis Ball	116	Whole group, circle	5-10 min	Easy
Text Tenses	128	Solo	10-20 min	Moderate
That Sinking Feeling	32	Whole group	5-15 min	Moderate
The Clapping Game	22	Whole group	5-10 min	Easy
The Quick One	102	Small groups	5-15 min	Easy
Three Circles	48	Solo, partners	5-15 min	Moderate
Three Words	50	Solo, partners	10-15 min	Moderate
Tracing Through Space	76	Solo	5-15 min	Moderate
Travelling in Pairs	72	Partners	5-10 min	Easy
Using Words	130	Solo, partners	10-20 min	Moderate
Visualisation	16	Partners	5-10 min	Moderate
Walk, Stop, Sit, Lie	84	Whole group, smaller groups	10-15 min	Easy/Moderate
Word Search	132	Partners	10-20 min	Moderate
Your Research Task	150	Solo	15-45 min	Moderate

PREFACE

Welcome to *More Dance Improvisations*. This book will provide you with interesting ideas that can be explored and experienced with movement. Dance improvisation is about discovery, taking risks and allowing yourself to come up with a variety of movement answers in the moment without judgment.

When making a dance piece, it can be difficult to picture what the final product will look like, what shape it will take and what the emphasis will be. These improvisations will give you the keys to unlock ideas you'll find useful on your choreographic journey. They can be used to collect movements for a whole dance composition or, in their basic form, to warm up, shake off the day and train yourself to challenge your dance skills and ideas.

All art starts from nothing – from an idea, a seed, a thought, something found or something that sparks interest. These games, tasks, ideas, stimuli and developments will give you or your students a little push to find creative vision, explore movement and discover how they can be developed, adapted and structured.

The first improvisations in chapter 2 have been called 'warm-up games' to inspire a sense of play, of beginning, of warming up and starting to move with ease. The mover shouldn't overthink their responses to these games. They're simply to introduce the space, the idea of moving, the other participants and the theme, as well as to set the scene for the rest of the session. You can use one or two at the start or, indeed, fill the entire session with games, depending on the needs, confidence levels and openness to play the movers have. Hopefully, they'll feel good during this positive playing without thinking too much about what movements look good on them or moving to impress. These games will develop quick thinking, group thinking, movement communication and an awareness of the needs and movements of others.

The next dance improvisations in the book are split into chapter 3: solo and duo ideas and chapter 4: group creative ideas. These are all kinaesthetic tasks. Practising dance improvisation, especially, with solo tasks is not always easy, and not all tasks suit all dancers. One way to help is to build up over time. If a group is struggling to create movement, start with a quick solo task and move on. Each improvisation task has a brief description, an image, numbered tasks for clarity, a teaching tip and ideas to take the task further or develop the idea where needed.

Chapter 5 explores creating dance that moves beyond kinaesthetic to aural stimulus-based improvisation tasks, so that sound, music, voice, text and the physical setting can serve as starting places for dance. It also includes the use of props and set.

Chapter 6 examines ways to develop the ideas and movements created in the previous chapters so dancers can think about the process leading to a product – a step towards composition. It provides clear descriptions of how to develop movement material and possible ways to structure dance.

This book is every dance teacher's companion, whether you're delivering for KS3, KS4 or Post 16 dance in schools or colleges in the United Kingdom or middle school through college in the United States. It will prove an invaluable source of creative ideas if you're a dance artist exploring your own professional practice. The improvisation tasks and exercises will encourage dancers' imaginative responses to a varied selection of stimuli, whether alone or groups.

All the tasks in this book have been tried and tested to ensure that your creative journey is successful. I hope this book encourages you to explore movement and dance with excitement and an awareness of the amazing things you can do.

Have fun,
Justine

ACKNOWLEDGEMENTS

Front image and all internal dance photographs by David McHugh. www.brightonpictures.com

Internal photographs with thanks to Andrea Davis and the dancers at The BRIT School for Performing and Creative Arts, United Kingdom. The BRIT School is the leading performing and creative arts school in the United Kingdom and is completely free to attend.

Thanks to the following for their support:
- One Dance UK
- Russell Maliphant
- Hannah Kirkpatrick
- Jane White, Course Leader, BA (Hons) Dance at Arts University Bournemouth
- Nicola Dominy
- Zoe Thompson
- Clive Peter Reeve
- Frida Augusta Reeve
- Greta Giulietta Reeve
- Caitlin E.G. Reeve
- Jasmine, Jardine and Jeremy
- Diane and John

chapter 1

Introduction and How to Use This Book

Because improvisation is a spontaneous pastime, it can lead you in surprising new directions. You can rely less on obvious ideas if you're willing to start moving without embarrassment or the need to be perfect on the first try. It's about letting go and immersing yourself in the moment of movement.

When you create choreography, it's important to know why you're doing it. This can mean the difference between good and ambiguous choreography. You can improve the success of a dance piece by understanding your stimulus, your theme, your intention, who your audience is and what you want from them. Knowing that your dance has purpose will drive your ideas.

The real key to using improvisational exploration for successful choreography is remembering the movements that feel authentic, vibrant, visceral and exciting. If you can remember how a movement felt and where it was performed in space, you can recall what worked. Because technology is so accessible, many choreographers and professional dance companies use video to capture their improvisations and select phrases and movement ideas they want to keep or develop. Companies such as the Russell Maliphant Dance Company in the United Kingdom, whom I had the privilege of observing in rehearsal, edit these improvisations into phrases and sequences that dancers subsequently learn. This speeds up the choreographic process, allowing them to improvise and not have to hold the movements in their memories until needed; it's all captured on film and can be assessed at any point. They can then focus on the emphasis of the task and build on the dynamics of the emotive responses they experienced.

As you and your students explore improvisations, try each task and be receptive to what happens. You can develop these ideas by using the suggestions in the Further Development sections or repeating the task to see if you come up with a different response. If you find that a task or idea in this book is working for you and you feel inspired, explore this in depth and transform it into something entirely yours. If, however, you struggle to find a movement answer, stop and move on to something else or adapt it however you see fit.

WARMING UP AND SAFE PRACTICE

Warming up through improvisation tasks allows dancers to begin a rehearsal with ideas transposed into their bodies. It's a great way to get in tune with how they move without imposing steps, exercises and counts. They can spend time on areas that need extra attention and make sure they work through their whole bodies. Dancers must be able to safely explore and not push themselves until they're warm enough.

For all the warm-ups and creative exploration tasks within this book, you'll need to provide a large, clear space suitable for practical movement tasks, such as a school hall, gym or dance studio. It's good practice for both teachers and students to wear dance clothes or a physical education kit. It's vital that dancers take part in a warm-up to raise their heart rate and address all the major muscle groups to help prevent injury. Warm-ups prepare students for the class ahead, and they're also fun!

Dancers will also need to cool down at the end of practical explorations and improvisation classes. Cool-downs gradually lower the heart rate, stretch major muscle groups and bring focus to the end of the class. They also provide an opportunity to reflect on creative ideas. You could use the warm-up movements to cool down, but it's important to slow the action down and then move into appropriate stretches.

In chapter 5, students are encouraged to use props and other objects to inspire movement. Please make sure you have up-to-date risk assessments in place and can advise of potential hazards.

You can also use the following Safe Studio checklist or create your own:

Size – Ensure that there's enough space to dance.

Airflow – Make sure the room is well ventilated.

Fire exits – Clearly mark all exits.

Ears – Set the music at a comfortable level.

Sprung floor – Provide an uncluttered, non-slippery sprung floor.

Temperature – Keep the temperature around 21 to 22 degrees Celsius (around 70 to 72 degrees Fahrenheit).

Uniform – Ensure that dancers dress appropriately.

Drinks – Keep drinks away from the floor to prevent spills.

Illuminate – Keep the room well lit.

Overhead – Make sure the room has high ceilings for safe jumps and lifts.

EFFECTIVE PLANNING

When planning your creative workshops and classes, you'll want to ensure that dancers have the best experience. Once you've planned a session, you can use the five I's to keep you on track: inspire, invigorate, inform, involve and include. I developed this philosophy to ensure that your workshop or lesson is as successful as it could be.

The first I is for 'inspire'. Teachers and leaders can encourage and remind students that dance is fun and that enjoyment is a key part of any dance pursuit. When you lead a dance activity, you can engage students and instantly observe their creative responses and energies that permeate the room. You can also decide in the moment if you need to add more detail or encouragement to get the most out of your dancers.

The second I is for 'invigorate'. Dance is good exercise and can provide amazing physical and mental health benefits. Invigorating sessions can improve cardiovascular fitness, bone health and weight management.

This leap can only be performed when all health and safety aspects are considered.

The third I is for 'inform'. When you lead a group of dancers, you have an opportunity to give them as much information as they can take in. This could be about dance practice, safety, creativity, other art practice or stimuli that can justify decisions and clarify intentions. Even the use of different terminology or dance vocabulary would allow dancers to discuss, describe and evaluate their own practice eloquently.

The fourth I is for 'involve'. Be aware of all students in your class or workshop and aim to get them dancing, creating, planning, rehearsing and sharing ideas with one another. Find ways to ensure that they feel part of the process and validate their ideas.

The last I is for 'include'. What is inclusive practice? It's finding a way to encourage your students to engage in dance and being flexible to accommodate their different needs. Therefore, you can make dance accessible by pre-empting and accepting, gathering information in advance, finding appropriate music and knowing the amazing impact it can have.

Important differences to support could be

- between individuals,
- based on cultural identity and what's important to us,
- aesthetics in different dance situations,
- reasons for participating in dance,
- learning needs amongst individuals and groups,
- methodologies and pedagogies to ensure that dancers have the most positive experience,
- physical differences that produce different dancing opportunities and solutions and
- contexts in which meaningful dance takes place.

Every dance teacher holds values that aren't random but are cultivated over years of diverse experiences. Bring these values to every lesson, session or workshop and trust that you know how to foster your students' curiosity.

You may find that some dancers will be natural movers but that others will find it awkward or silly. Here are a few tips that might encourage and support every dancer:

- Encourage individual interpretations. They may not all be the same or produce expected movement outcomes.
- Value their movement ideas.
- Emphasise that not everyone is expected to be the same.
- Regularly praise and recognise their talents and efforts.
- Yes, again. Give them time to practise and rehearse if they need it.

Inclusion isn't about political or cultural trends. It's about valuing each member of your dance class, responding to their needs and utilizing their potential. Look at who you have in your class. Who has turned up? Who has elected to take your dance class? Who is new to dance? It's not about who isn't there.

The drive to make dance classes and workshops accessible and diverse to encourage enrolment is a just one. In recent years, a growing concern has been the possible lingering effects of exclusion. While classes may contain lessons that don't reflect students' cultures, needs, skills and desires, it's an ongoing learning curve. Your gift as a dance teacher is to inspire, understand and anticipate.

Dance is for everyone. There's a variety of ways to provide this opportunity for all, like creating simple adaptations for tasks. If you have dancers out with injuries, they can still share ideas or aid rehearsals by giving direction and praise to other dancers. Once you've completed your lesson plan, workshop plan or scheme of learning, take a moment to check that it's inclusive. Reflecting on your planning as well as your outcome will help you grow as a dance facilitator and ensure that you deliver high-quality dance experiences.

This would be a good time to check that you've included the 5 I's in your preparations.

Dance students receive tips for successful improvisation.

TOP TIPS FOR DANCE IMPROVISATION

When using these improvisations, please remember that you can never exhaust ideas. There are many ways to set and reuse different improvisation tasks and endless stimuli for composing dance pieces. Anything that inspires or excites students to make movements that suit their dance is a good starting point. Allow them the opportunity to explore their ideas without judgement and insist that there's no wrong movement answer. The more time and space they're given to explore moving this way, the more unique and innovative they'll be. If they're open to trying new improvisational tasks, they can discover new things and freely develop movement ideas. Improvisation is really structured play, wherein dancers have the chance to be absorbed in the creative process.

PLANNING YOUR WORKSHOP

Once you have an idea or theme you want to focus on in the session, you can select improvisations from each chapter in any combination. Begin your workshop or class with a warm-up from chapter 2 to raise the heart rate and mentally prepare dancers for creative activities. Then, move on to the creative exploration tasks found in chapters 3, 4 and 5. These tasks are designed to develop choreographic processes and generate dance phrases and sequences for compositional pieces, depending on where dancers are in their own processes. When they're ready, they can explore the developments and rehearsal considerations from chapter 6.

Here are a few plans to give you a balanced session on a given theme. You can, of course, adapt these as needed:

Workshop 1 – Topic: Creating Meaningful Duets
- Sending a Message
- Drawing Whilst Supported

Workshop 2 – Topic: Using Set
- Pointing Game

Workshop 3 – Topic: Using Music
- Repetitive Dance

Workshop 4 – Topic: Narrative Dance
- Make Some Noise
- Pick Three Words

Workshop 5 – Topic: Cyberspace
- Sending a Message

Workshop 6 – Topic: Journeys
- Applaud the Stars
- Making Maps

Workshop 7 – Plastic in the Oceans
- Struggle

The following improvisations work well for new groups: Snap, At the Same Time, Someone's Coming and Travelling in Pairs.

The following introduce movement and dance to new groups: Running to the Middle, Applaud the Stars and Walk, Sit, Stop, Lie.

The following are good for more experienced groups: That Sinking Feeling, Swing Time, Visualisation, Falling Through Centre, Drawing Whilst Supported, Lighting Line and Connection Perfection.

FINDING THE RIGHT MUSIC

What should you look for in music for your choreographic work? Are you looking for inspiration or something that works with movement ideas you already have? Are you looking for something that fits within a theme or exam question? Music is a helpful tool that sets the tone or mood in the studio during lessons, workshops and performances.

Choosing music is an exciting prospect, but finding something appropriate can be time consuming. You're looking for music that will inspire movement design or music that will complement what you've already created. To do this and be true to your artistic vision, intention and themes, you might have to forget your audience and peers and simply trust yourself. Of course, you, as the teacher, will have fantastic insight into what may work. Therefore, you can look for anything that appeals to you and makes you want to create, move and dance. Listen to every track and make note of the ones that inspire you. Next, you could try motifs or phrases you've created with each track you've marked. If you've chosen the right one, the music will play from start to finish without giving anyone in the audience a chance to remember that they're part of an audience.

Below are questions to consider when choosing:

- Does it evoke the right mood or atmosphere?
- Does it support the theme of the dance?

- Is it from a particular era or in a style that suits the dance?
- Could it suggest a location?
- Does it have a structure you can follow?
- What instruments are playing and how can you use these features?
- With which parts or instruments will you correlate?
- What relationships will the dance have with the music?

Before using any of the improvisations in this book, arm yourself with a diverse selection of music. Keep a folder, playlist, or box of CDs you've listened to. You may want to make note of emotions, dynamics or what the music could accomplish so you can play the right track at the right time.

WHAT IS MUSICALITY?

Musicality is the awareness of music, rhythm and how dancers express these with their bodies. Musicality in dance has two main components: openness and originality. Musical openness is the ability to receive, comprehend and be sensitive to musical concepts like rhythm, tempo, phrasing and mood. Musical originality is the ability to connect with accompanying music, interpret it and add movement dynamics that relate to it in a unique way.

Musicality in dance, then, is the degree to which dancers are open and original in their translations of music through movement. Teachers can establish greater openness and originality by providing plenty of practice. Musicality starts the moment you move to music. As you warm up or perform class exercises in your training, you're exhibiting musicality.

Listen, Listen – Then Dance

When you choreograph to a novel piece of music, listening is key. If you improvise, you'll select and refine your choices in the moment and your responses will be immediate. It's a good idea to film and watch these responses because there may be moments you'd like to keep. Remember, musicality comes in many forms and there's no right or wrong way to interpret a score. You may choose to choreograph to a track that challenges you. In that case, don't be intimidated. Listen to that piece repeatedly. The better you know a piece of music, the more you'll be able to play with the dynamics of movement instead of always dancing on the beat. Which qualities could you emphasise in your movements? Try to identify all the instruments, make notes and draw pictures. Visualise the music and how you might dance to it.

Play

Experiment with just moving to music anywhere and everywhere. You could do this with your eyes closed in a space with no hazards. Try setting a playlist to shuffle.

Explore Speed

Slower music can give students more time to explore, play and try different styles. Play a piece of slower music and use it to inspire movements to cross the dance studio diagonally. You could also try a faster track to push creativity.

Keep It Simple

Often, dance students who concentrate on technical aspects of the class won't be as sensitive to qualities of the music. You could assign simple exercises they can master quickly so they can take the time to listen and respond to musical subtleties.

Variety Is the Spice

Vary the music you use from class to class. This will force dancers to listen and develop their musicality skills. You could make them aware of specific qualities of the music, such as speed, emotion or intensity and how they can express these qualities through their movements.

Discuss the Music

Musicality is instinctive for some teachers, professional dancers and dance students, but it can also be learned. Take time in class to discuss the music with students. Ask them questions about what they hear, how it makes them want to move and what meaning it gives their movements. Ask them to reflect on any movement changes after the discussion.

Don't Hold Your Breath

Music can encourage you to breathe correctly. Ask dancers not to hold their breaths throughout a phrase or piece. Try to relate their breathing to the musical patterns.

COMPONENTS OF MUSIC AND THEIR RELATIONSHIP TO DANCE

Music can inspire dance, where the movement relates and responds to the rhythm, melody, tempo, dynamics, beat, harmony, duration, style and even the texture. The dance movements might relate to just one or indeed all these key components.

The Aural Setting

Whilst music is often described as the aural setting, this term also relates to other auditory possibilities that can be used to successfully accompany dance.

Types of accompaniments include
- *music* – pre-recorded or live,
- *sound score* – sound 'effects', environmental, naturalistic,
- *found sound* – breath and body sounds whilst dancing,
- *voice* – song, words, breath sounds and
- *silence*.

The Most Popular Collaboration Is, of Course, Dance and Music

What the audience experiences with their eyes and ears should match and, in some way, support each other. This compatibility can also include contrasts, which could create interesting moments of juxtaposition.

The phrases and sequences of movement you've created as part of your choreography will have their own form and structure, with high points that can be emphasised using sound. Using music to create atmosphere can make some moments more vibrant and enhance the relationship between dancer and sound.

What Are the Components of Music? What Can You Expect to Hear?

When listening to a piece of music for the first time you might initially respond to several of the components listed below, but if you read this list and then listened you may discover more. As a choreographer, your research also includes listening to your choice of aural setting multiple times.

Components of music include
- Time signature (beats per bar – e.g., 3/4 or 4/4 are the most popular)
- Instruments (e.g., keyboard, guitar and drums)
- Rhythm and polyrhythm, which is more than one rhythm at the same time
- Accents (e.g., stressed notes)
- Key signature (e.g., major or minor)
- Tempo, speed and beats per minute (BPM)
- Melodies and tunes that can be layered, combined or separated
- Harmony or discordance (creating atmosphere)
- Pitch (e.g., high or low in the scale)
- Pauses (silence)
- Polyphony: two or more melodies or voices
- Dynamics (e.g., fluid or staccato)
- Climax: a build-up of tension, sound and loudness
- Structure (e.g., AB, ABA and rondo)

This list is not exhaustive. Explore music theory to see what else you can learn.

RELATIONSHIPS THAT DANCE CAN HAVE WITH MUSIC

Dance and music can exist together in different ways. Some of these ways are so obvious that you can take away the sound and guess the tempo and time signature, whereas other dance pieces give you no clues. These relationships that dance can have with music are not necessarily meant to be separate ideas; they can be used all together for one piece of music if you are up for that challenge. This list is to help inspire and inform you to make choices in your movement actions, reactions, ideas and developments within your own choreography.

Direct Correlation

This occurs when movement and music work together to mirror each other. For example, if there are softer moments in the music, the dance will also have softer, smaller or slower movements. It's often referred to as 'Mickey

Mousing'. The best example of this can be seen in Disney's *Fantasia*, where the movements and characters, including Mickey, work directly with the musical score by matching sounds with actions. If this is how you want to use your music, this film is worth a watch.

Music Visualisation

This is where the dance can become a visual picture of what's being heard. This is referred to as 'hearing the dance and seeing the music'. It can follow elements of the music, such as melody, tempo and accents. If you close your eyes, listen to a piece of music and use your imagination, what can you visualise? Some classical pieces make you think of things like mountains, the sea, a storm or a flower opening. This phenomenon is seen in ballet pieces such as *Swan Lake* and *Romeo and Juliet*. In *Romeo and Juliet*, different pieces of music are used for the mood of different scenes. In the part where Juliet dances with her nurse, there's a different melody for each of their characteristics. Try listening to the music of a dance piece first before watching it.

Mutual Coexistence

This is when the dance holds its own identity against the music. Neither the music nor the dance is dominant, and they each have their individual strengths and importance. They may have a similar underlying theme but may not always interact. Interestingly, this can relieve the dance from its musical dependence so it can be performed to different pieces with a similar time signature. This is useful if you want to make the dance first and find the music when you feel ready.

Call and Response

This is often referred to as 'question and answer', where the music plays a rhythm or melody and the dance matches with a response, like an echo. For example, a master drummer could use calls to signal dancers to change steps. It can also work the other way round; for example, in some forms of Indian dance, the musicians watch the dancer and change the music when the movement changes.

Disassociation

Music and dance are often created to exist independently of each other. The music and movements exist only for themselves. They don't take cues from or respond to each other. Perhaps the music and dance only come together in performance, as choreographer Merce Cunningham often demonstrated with his company in New York. Unlike the other relationships, disassociation can produce amazing chance results but can be hard to watch if there are no dynamic changes to keep interest. It can produce 'arty' dance.

WHAT IS A PHRASE?

A 'phrase' could be described as the smallest unit of dance. It has a beginning, middle and end. It also contains a high point. You may ask: Why not just perform unphrased movement? Unphrased movement isn't difficult to do, but it's dull to watch because phrasing occurs naturally in life, as in art. The high point could be described as the most important part of the phrase. It may be a faster or stronger movement, higher or lower jump or fall, extreme change or sudden stop. Not all phrases have obvious high points; we'd be worn out if we were constantly bombarded with high points as dancers and viewers.

The term 'choreographic phrase' is often confused with 'movement combinations'. Most dancers take technique classes before beginning to choreograph and assume that the short movement combinations they learned are the same as phrases. Movement combinations can be movements strung together like beads without notice of their individual shape, colour, texture or relationship to each other. They're often used to train dancers. That doesn't mean that longer sequences performed at the end of the class aren't phrases. Try asking students which exercises they consider to be phrased. Choreographic phrases convey images, feelings and ideas through visual impressions, stories, symbols and design elements. With or without actual meaning, it's expressive; it has flesh, whereas a movement combination only has bones.

chapter

2

Warm-Up Games and Improvisations

This chapter explores the concepts of play and spontaneous movement as stimuli for warming up the body and preparing the mind for new experiences. The games and improvisations within will prepare dancers for the creative tasks ahead, improve reaction times and explore key features of movement.

You can select one warm-up task before embarking on the next step in your workshop or use several to build relationships and group experiences. You could use Running to the Middle to get students engaged in the space and then move into The Clapping Game. The idea is to ignite dancers' creativity but not to exhaust them with too many warm-ups.

Each task includes a description, teaching tips and further developments you can enjoy in class or build on in subsequent workshops. For example, Repetitive Dance can be used at the beginning of any class with different music and formations for as long as necessary. Snap could help dancers begin to move and discover partners. It could then be linked to a duo creative task from chapter 3.

VISUALISATION

This is a warm-up to mobilise the body and help dancers think about responding to direction. Ask them to form pairs and find space in the studio away from others. Ask them to discuss and perform the following warm-ups with their partners. They can respond however they wish; there's no wrong or right way. You could demonstrate or read this list with dancers facing each other.

1. Spread your toes on the floor and find a firm base on which to stand.

2. Soften your knees and gently pulse. Then gradually come to a stop.

3. Stretch your arms up to the ceiling, out to the sides and then down to the floor, bending the torso and dropping the head.

4. Find a way back up to standing with your head leading, perhaps creating a spatial pathway that curves or spirals.

5. Stretch one arm up to the ceiling and try extending beyond what you'd normally do. Circle the arm, reaching as far as you can.

6. Try with the other arm, perhaps in different directions.

7. Extend your arm to draw a wide circle round your body.

8. Find a way for the arm to spiral. This could be bending the elbow, dropping and circling the arm.

9. Find a movement that incorporates the torso and legs. Fluidly explore a range of movements that induce the same feeling of spiralling, dropping and circling.

Chapter 2 – Warm-Up Games and Improvisations   17

Paired dancers respond to their partners' verbal descriptions of the warm-up.

Teaching Tip

Encourage students to safely explore the notion of play. Emphasize that there are no wrong movement answers and no expectations for the movements to be interesting to watch. Remind them that they're simply warming up and exploring their personal movement ranges.

Further Development

Dancers could create their own warm-up using a series of simple instructions like the list provided. In addition, have them work with their partners to warm up the shoulders, hips and spine in different ways.

POINTING GAME

This is a great starter game to help dancers begin to move round the space and become aware of what's in the room. It also challenges them to speak whilst moving and to consider how they might translate words into movement.

1. Ask each dancer to point to the door, a window, the floor, another dancer or anything else they want to spot. You could specify how close they should be to the object or person they choose.

2. Instruct them to walk round the room in any direction and continue pointing out objects they see out loud. Make sure they're not colliding or all walking the same way.

3. Have them continue to travel but to alternate between walking, running or galloping. This will encourage them to become more dynamic and their voices may become louder so they can be heard.

4. Ask dancers to point to the object, say its name and create a movement for it. They could outline the shape, move to the object's level or perform a gesture that, in some way, represents the object to them. Allow them time to explore this.

5. Direct them to pair up and take each other round the room with one partner leading the other as they point, speak and perform their actions. They can decide who will perform and who will copy so they can move together. They could also explore a balance between who's being copied and who's leading.

6. Dancers could silently speed up their actions so they're moving quickly round the room whilst avoiding each other. To provide a sense of performance, half the class could observe.

Dancers walk whilst pointing and describing their environment.

Teaching Tip

When groups are asked to walk round a space in any direction whilst completing another task, they usually start walking in the same direction. Bring their attention to where they're travelling and guide them to move independently. They also observe what others are doing as they gauge what actions to use to bring their chosen objects to life. You could stop and watch a few or discuss their techniques. If dancers are struggling, they could use a movement that begins with the same letter (e.g., floor – fall, wall – wriggle or leg – lunge).

Further Development

Explore using bigger groups of three, four and five dancers copying each other. This can be amusing to watch.

APPLAUD THE STARS

This improvisation game focuses on warming dancers up whilst working on performance, focus and the ensemble concept. They'll need to be aware of each other and avoid collisions.

1. Ask dancers to walk anywhere in the space but to balance it out so that no one is isolated at any one point. Encourage them to fill gaps and be aware of where other dancers are. You could stop them and point out areas where there are no dancers to highlight this.

2. Once you've explained what their movement response will be, dancers will need to respond quickly to the following instructions, which you can call out in any order:

- 'Applaud': Clap hands together. You can decide if this is one clap or several.
- 'Floor': Find a smooth transition down into the floor.
- 'Sky': Reach for the sky and move out of the floor or rise and focus upwards.
- 'Stars': Perform a jump, hop or leap to reach for the stars. Decide if this is one jumping action or several.
- 'Stop' and 'go': Move or be still. You can decide if 'go' is running or another way of travelling, chosen by each dancer.

3. After saying these words in any order for an appropriate length of time, you can pass control to the dancers so they call out. Make sure they keep moving until they hear the next command.

4. Swap these instructions round so 'stop' becomes 'go' and 'go' becomes 'stop'. This will require them to concentrate on what they're doing.

Dancers find a smooth transition into the floor.

Teaching Tip

If your instructions are clear, students won't be caught by surprise. Ask them to be aware of what the rest of the group is doing. If they're aware, you'll find that step 3 is more successful because they'll begin to move as an ensemble.

Further Development

In pairs, dancers can travel round the room and simply focus on each other. One person can decide which command to perform and their partner can respond:
- If one applauds, the other jumps for the stars.
- If one goes into the floor, the other reaches for the sky.
- If one travels round the space, the other stops or contrasts in a manner of their choosing.

THE CLAPPING GAME

This is a good warm-up game to help dancers think and respond quickly. It also introduces the concept of making a sound whilst moving. This is a whole group warm-up in which everyone will have an opportunity to move and observe each other.

1. Ask dancers to form a circle, facing inwards.

2. Instruct them to send a clap round the circle, first in one direction and then the other.

3. Have them change direction and send the clap back the other way. It helps if they perform the clap towards the person to whom they're passing it.

4. Ask them to send the clap across the circle and to avoid confusion by looking and clapping directly towards the person.

5. Have dancers send the clap round or across the circle. The idea is to keep it going and, perhaps, to see if they can increase their speed.

6. Ask them to walk out of the circle and round the room, passing a clap to someone on their travels.

7. Instruct them to run round the room and dodge each other whilst passing claps.

8. Direct them back to the circle. This time, when they pass the sound round and across, they must acknowledge that they've received it by performing a turn or jump. Then they can direct the sound to another dancer.

9. Ask students to move round the room, receive claps, perform jumps or turns and then send the claps on.

Dancers send the clapping action round the circle.

Teaching Tip

You can try each part as many times as you need to help dancers focus and develop a quick response. You can add steps in each workshop so they can build up this task over time. If they find steps 6 and 7 confusing, have a command to direct them back into the circle to start again, making it clear which dancer will start the action.

Further Development

Dancers could explore walking, galloping or running to travel into and out of the circle whilst passing the clap sound. They could also find ways to make other sounds pass to each other. Further, you could swap the clap for any dance action or combination of actions.

DOUBLE NUMBERS

This quick warm-up game is beneficial to new groups in a new space. Students will be running and dodging, so please ensure that the floor, footwear or bare feet aren't slippery.

1. Ask dancers to walk or run round the room, avoiding collisions with each other and using the whole space.

2. Shout out a number they must form groups of as quickly as possible without talking. You can count down from five or ten to give them time to complete the task.

3. Ask them to travel round the room again as in step 1 but to keep moving.

4. Give the group two numbers: one for the number of dancers per group and another they must arrange their bodies to represent. For example, for the numbers four and eight, a group of four dancers would create the number eight. Dancers must attempt this without talking to promote observation and creativity.

5. Ask them to quickly comment on what worked and what didn't.

6. Travel again, say another two numbers and discuss.

7. Have students add levels to these actions. For example, they could have three people form the number nine at a low level.

8. Experiment with location (e.g., stage right or left).

Dancers arrange themselves into the shape of a number as a group.

Teaching Tip

This is a quick game that will encourage listening and problem solving in the moment. You can layer on steps 7 and 8 in a subsequent session so students can master immediate response.

Further Development

You can continue to layer on as many other factors as the group can handle. You may have to build on this over several sessions to accumulate skills. You could include planes (e.g., horizontal or vertical) or connections with body parts. You can replace the second number with an action, like gesture, jump, travel, turn, fall or balance.

MAKE SOME NOISE

This warm-up game will help students think quickly and make movement choices in the moment. It also introduces the notion of making a sound whilst moving. Although this isn't a difficult task, it may suit more mature groups.

1. Ask dancers to form a large circle.

2. Go round the circle and ask them to place a hand on a body part and make any sound. Hopefully, as you go, all the sounds will be different. For example, they can beep when touching their heads or gasp when touching their shoulders.

3. If this works well, try once more and ask dancers to make a different noise with a new body part. Sounds can be higher pitched, longer or use more breath.

4. Ask them to create three sound and body combinations in a row (e.g., beep and head, gasp and shoulder or click and knee).

5. Go round the circle and ask each student to share their three sounds and movements.

6. Have them create a rhythmical version, which can have repeated, staccato and longer sounds. It will be easier if they use the three they've already made. Have they made a dance tune?

One dancer in the circle shares their three movements and three sounds.

Teaching Tip

Ask dance partners to observe each other, discuss what they felt looked effective and then have another go. You can have them copy the actions from steps 2 and 4 or send them in a canon round the circle.

Further Development

In pairs, dancers could learn each others' sounds to make a longer phrase with six sounds. Then, they could decide where to face and change the direction throughout. They could try making the sound as their partners touch them on an agreed-upon body part. Again, they'll need to refine the rhythm and add in repeats to make it a tune.

SNAP

This game helps dancers spot movements quickly and be aware of each other. You can use a known sequence or teach them five simple movements as they enter the space. These could include gestures and shapes.

1. Divide a known sequence into five movements or teach five new ones, each lasting the same number of counts (e.g., 'one and a two').

2. Ask dancers to run, gallop, walk or roll round the room. Ask them to select and remember one of the five movements they learned. On the command 'pair', have them find partners and stand facing them.

3. On the command 'dance', have them dance the movement they've chosen from the five. If they dance the same movement, they shout 'snap' and sit down.

4. Repeat steps 2 and 3 until you have one pair left.

5. Have this last pair choose a movement. Ask all other dancers to stand up and select one as well. Finally, have everyone dance their own movement and determine if it's the same as the last pair and if any others are performing it.

Mirroring each other's actions, partners shout 'snap' and sit down.

Teaching Tip

Encourage dancers to vary the movements they select and not simply perform the one they most easily remember. They must remain focused on the game in order to get back up and participate in step 5.

Further Development

You can increase the number of movements from which dancers can choose. You can also allocate a movement to each card from a deck for the next class, and hand each student a card before they start the game.

SWING TIME

This warm-up will articulate the arms, shoulders and spine. In a circle, or using a given front, students can explore a variety of swinging gestures with their arms. These actions will employ all three planes: vertical, horizontal and sagittal (e.g., door, table and wheel). This style of contemporary dance emphasises the relationship between swing, impulse and impact and breath, body weight and gravity. Explore each step before asking dancers to form pairs and create their own warm-up to music.

1. Ask dancers to extend both arms above their heads in a parallel high position, then circle them forwards, back behind the body and back to parallel high, completing a full circle. This action can also be reversed so the arms travel backwards. Dancers who feel able to can add knee bends at the point where their arms fall and could explore swinging one arm at a time before joining both arms.

2. Ask them to further develop their swinging actions by bending their torsos as their arms drop. As they circle their arms back, they should return to a standing position. They can try this action with or without knee bends.

3. Dancers can add in four knee bends or pliés in parallel and drop the torso. Instruct them to circle their arms forwards from parallel high. Once their arms are down by their sides, they can bend and then straighten their knees as they swing back up. When they drop their arms on the second circle, have them reverse their direction, bending their torsos and knees again. When students are bent with their heads looking through their legs, have them straighten their knees and continue circling backwards to bring the body up to a standing position. They can complete another knee bend once they're upright whilst they circle both arms backwards.

4. Ask them to explore swinging their arms on the horizontal, or table, plane. They should swing their arms horizontally from side to side, wrapping them round their bodies and extending them as they swing. Emphasise the stretching of the arms before they flex them round the body.

5. Have dancers explore swinging their arms on the vertical, or door, plane. They should reach both arms up diagonally and let them swing down to the side, front, and opposite high diagonal. They can also swing from side to side. They could perform this movement in second position in turnout, and plié when both arms come across low in front of their bodies.

Dancers explore swinging and circling both arms.

6. Have students explore swinging actions with one arm at a time. Ask them to circle one arm on the vertical plane, starting from parallel high. Also try the other two planes, switching arms and adding a step with the arm movement.

Teaching Tip

The proper use of breath is also important when moving, especially when performing swing actions that incorporate gravity. Discuss the points in the swing action when dancers should breathe in and out to enhance their movements.

Further Development

Have dancers form pairs and create their own warm-ups incorporating these swing actions. Set a time frame or number of counts and have them perform the warm-up to music. Once they've mastered their warm-ups, they should be able to lead the whole class through one.

THAT SINKING FEELING

This improvisation task requires dancers to consider levels and dynamics. You could play 'stuck in the mud' to warm them up prior to assigning it.

1. Instruct dancers to travel across the room as if they're travelling through mud, whatever that may mean to them. They could perform this in lines so they have enough space to explore.

2. Ask them to find two or three different ways of sinking into the floor. They could, perhaps, imagine they're moving through thick mud and all their bones have turned to liquid.

3. Ask them to travel across the room again, this time adding their sinking movements.

4. Challenge dancers to get as low as possible.

5. Ask them to find two or three different ways to pull themselves up out of the floor with the same weighty quality as if it's difficult.

6. Again, direct them to travel across the room, this time adding their sinking and pulling movements into and out of the floor.

Dancers explore sinking into the floor as they travel across the dance space.

Teaching Tip

There should be no time or count limit on how long it takes dancers to go into or out of the floor, unless you want to set one. They can also move along the floor before pulling themselves up to standing.

Further Development

This could develop into a new warm-up in which dancers travel, sink, reemerge and continue travelling. You could add that if a dancer spends too long on the floor, another has to try to pull them out of the mud. You could ask half the group to observe the other and discuss possible meanings.

AT THE SAME TIME

This is a great warm-up to help dancers with their performance skills, especially their awareness of each other on stage.

1. Have dancers walk round the space, occupying it evenly.

2. Ask them to complete the following instructions at the same time:

- Stop and find a moment of stillness.
- Go into the floor.
- Touch your nose.
- Rise out of the floor.
- Balance on one leg.
- Clap.
- Travel round the room.
- Jump.

The goal here is for dancers to work as an ensemble. Therefore, they must use eye contact, a slow pace and spatial awareness to complete the tasks at the same time.

3. Split the class into groups of four or five. Have them add two more actions to the list and use each command at least once (e.g., have everyone turn at the same time). They can allocate one person to call out the commands.

4. Keeping students in their small groups, have everyone perform the commands at the same time but without anyone calling out instructions.

Chapter 2 – Warm-Up Games and Improvisations

Dancers work together to balance at the same time.

Teaching Tip

You may have to allow for minor variation at first, but push dancers to complete the tasks in unison. You might want to add step 4 when using this improvisation again with a group.

Further Development

Once dancers have understood this task and tried step 4 in smaller groups, you could go back to having the whole class move together but without prompting. They could also try performing a phrase or known sequence whilst they have this improved awareness of each other.

SOMEONE'S COMING!

This game can be used to help dancers listen and react quickly to commands and ideas. Instruct them to walk round and evenly fill the space using interesting pathways. This improvisation game works well if you accompany it with music (perhaps from a film score).

Ask everyone to respond to these commands:

- 'Clear the space': Run to the nearest wall and press against it as hard as possible.
- 'Come together': Run to the middle of the room and attempt to take up as little space as possible.
- 'Artwork statue': Strike a pose like a statue.
- 'Dance style walk': Travel round the space as a dancer in any style.
- 'Conceal': Pretend to hide in the space without hiding (e.g., by covering the face or hiding behind someone else).
- 'Slow motion': Walk in slow motion or at different speeds.
- 'Someone's coming!': Drop to the floor and lie down as quickly as possible.

Dancers explore slow motion and concealing.

Teaching Tip

Students may use the commands competitively, but the game is more useful as a whole group activity.

Further Development

Dancers can add their own commands so the game grows each time they play. It can be interesting to split the class into smaller groups and have each play separately. You could also add a forfeit command if the groups find themselves in the same position as others. For example, if all dancers are on the floor after hearing 'someone's coming', then perhaps they can all jump in and out of the floor five times.

QUALITY

This warm-up requires dancers to explore the quality of movements on their own and as part of a group. It's better suited to dancers who can keep moving and trying ideas.

1. Ask dancers to move round the room continuously. Have them think about being fluid, ongoing, stepping, reaching, turning, falling, rising and never-ending.

2. As they move and improvise, ask them to bring their attention to the muscles used for each action. Encourage them to move whilst thinking and locating the muscles they're using.

3. Ask students to think about their bones and how they're moving through the space. Ask them to pay attention to the lines and how they're carving space with their bones.

4. Bring awareness to the surface of their skin as they move. Ask how it feels as they dance and if they can feel their way through the space.

5. Assess whether they can now travel through the space, as in step 1, and identify the muscles, bones and surfaces of their bodies used in all movements.

Dancers consider how visualising their skeleton moving changes the quality of their movements.

Teaching Tip

Dancers could write their findings in a logbook or choreographic diary. They could use drawings or film to highlight their explorations as evidence for assignments and projects.

Further Development

You could prompt dancers to discuss or think about the following question: How do you let the whole body come along for the journey of one action? They could find a picture of the skeletal system and begin to label the bones and muscles. Further, they can investigate muscle contraction and describe which muscles are used in a plié or jump.

SENDING A MESSAGE

This energetic game will help new groups warm up in a new space. Students will be running and dodging, so please ensure that the floor, footwear or bare feet aren't slippery.

1. Ask them to quickly run round the room in any direction and be aware of the space they're travelling through to avoid collisions.

2. Ask them to imagine they're messages flying through cyberspace. Ask them to create complicated floor paths if they can.

3. Have them stop and make a quick movement to resemble a message, like a jump, fall or gesture.

4. Without letting anyone know, have each student pick another person in the room to receive their dance message.

5. When you say 'send', have students run along their complicated pathways and deliver their dance message to the person they've chosen.

Dancers send an imagined message to each other in movement.

Teaching Tip

Ask dancers to observe each other to see if they've received the message. Can they demonstrate with movement that they received it?

Further Development

This is a great exercise to watch, and you could split the class in half so dancers can watch each other. You can add other movements to the message, such as text.

REPETITIVE DANCE

This improvisation uses repetitive response to music as a device to warm dancers up. You'll need a selection of upbeat music to accompany this task.

1. Direct dancers to form a large circle as quickly as possible.

2. Play an upbeat piece of music and ask them to copy you as you perform a repetitive dance step that fits with the music's style, tempo and mood. As long as the movements are repeated, they can include isolated body parts or simple step patterns.

3. Call a dancer to the middle to start a new step that everyone can follow. Continue until the next dancer demonstrates their new step to follow.

4. Repeat until everyone has shared or the group is warm and ready for the next activity.

A dancer in the middle of the circle moves to upbeat music whilst others copy in real time.

Teaching Tip

Most dancers will enjoy this task and rise to the challenge. Explain to those who shy away from leading that they only need to perform a simple movement that can be repeated.

Further Development

You can repeat this activity in lines with one student facing the class. Each time you select a new dancer to follow, have them come to the front or the group turn to face them. They could also work in pairs by facing each other with one leading and the other following. They can switch frequently without stopping.

RUNNING TO THE MIDDLE

This is a great whole group warm-up to increase connections as well as heart rates. Because it's quick and simple, you could use it at the beginning of a workshop to bring everyone together.

1. Ask the whole class to form a large circle using the maximum amount of space available and face the middle.

2. At any point, you could ask one dancer to initiate a run to the middle. When they do, have everyone else copy them.

3. Once they're in the middle, ask them to continue running on the spot until someone initiates a run backwards into the large circle.

4. Repeat this warm-up as if waves are breaking on a shoreline.

5. You can add other actions once dancers reach the middle, such as stretches, yoga sun salutations, lunges or any other movements that can be copied.

Dancers run towards and away from the middle of the circle, producing a ripple effect.

Teaching Tip

Dancers should not be able to observe who initiates the run forwards or backwards. The idea is for them to move as an ensemble with a clear awareness of each other.

Further Development

In another session, you could adapt this task for smaller groups. Dancers can form a circle and travel round the room together, trying to maintain formation. During this time, one can stop suddenly. When they do, the whole group must also stop at the same time and anyone can restart the running. You can also replace running with any other travel technique or known dance sequence.

chapter 3

Solo and Duo Improvisations

This chapter explores the movement responses dancers can generate on their own and with partners. Through these tasks, they'll discover spontaneous movement answers that will develop, challenge and refine their creative responses, solo or in duos. Ensure that they're warm and ready to explore their movements in a space that complies with health and safety standards.

Dancers may want to document their ideas and findings, perhaps in a choreographic journal or video recording. Video would be especially useful to capture discoveries in the moment that can't be committed to memory. Mirrors can help with recall, but you may want to cover them at first so students aren't initially self-conscious or restricted by an outside aesthetic. They can take as long as they want to perform a task, especially if they're engaged, generating material and having fun.

You'll also find that sharing movements and engaging in discussions will aid students' creative processes, allowing them to explain choices, describe favourite moments and explore next steps. Effective questions include: What did they enjoy? What did they find challenging? What might they edit out? Which movements or ideas would they refine?

THREE CIRCLES

This is a simple yet effective solo task to help dancers think about using parts of their bodies to carve pathways through space. Make sure they're warm, ready and open to being creative.

1. Ask dancers to pick three parts of their bodies (e.g., elbow, head and hand).

2. Instruct them to draw a circle with the first part and think about the size, plane and level they've chosen. For example, they could make a large circle with an elbow on a vertical plane and low level.

3. Have them draw another circle with the second part. This time, it should contrast with the first circle in size, plane, level or even speed. They could change where it's performed in the studio or which way they're facing.

4. The third circle can contrast or complement the other two actions.

5. Ask dancers to join these three actions to create a short phrase. Have them consider how to transition from one to another to keep it one continuous phrase.

6. They could perform their phrases for each other in pairs. Ask them to decide where the front is and the best viewing direction.

7. Ask them to find a way to fit their phrases together. If they're working alone, they could create a second phrase to avoid when performing.

8. Ask dancers to add a third phrase using their own idea. For example, they could change all the levels or planes, contrast all their actions or perform each one in a different part of the room, creating a travelling transition.

One dancer draws a circle with their head and the other with a whole arm.

Teaching Tip

Stop and observe some of the partners to see if they can share any pointers that are working for them.

Further Development

Dancers could use their responses to each other from step 6 to see how the phrases can complement each other with a new partner or in a small group. They could develop two phrases together. One would fit movements together as they interlock or fill the space round each other. The other would allow them to complement each other's actions. This improvisation can also be completed using three arcs, three squares or three figure eights.

THREE WORDS

This is a good solo task to help students create movement material that promotes consideration of what's moving and how. They should be warm and ready to explore.

Cut

Rise

Slice

Melt

Dive

Scurry

Recoil

Shoot

Ask dancers to pick three words from this list to inspire three movements to perform with three body parts. For example, they could cut with an elbow, shoot with a foot or rise with the pelvis.

1. Have them join the movements with a transition, challenging them to take up as much space as possible.

2. Once it's become one phrase, have them add the dynamics they think will make each movement more effective. These can be exaggerated. They'll then add a static version.

3. Ask students to explore travelling these movements in a straight line to create a moving version.

4. They can join the static and moving versions to create a phrase or join all the movements in any order.

5. Once they're confident with this phrase, ask them to create a second by finding movements that oppose each one.

6. They can also join these to create a longer phrase to use in a solo or group dance.

Two dancers explore the words 'slice' and 'rise'.

Teaching Tip

Ask dancers to share what they've created for number 5 with the rest of the group. Prompt them to explain how they've placed the movements together and in what order. This will inspire others to reassess their responses.

Further Development

Ask dancers to find a way to make it travel. Have them challenge their partners to a race to see who can cover the most space whilst maintaining their choreographed movements. They could repeat this task but select words from a theme or idea to choreograph a whole dance. This could be from a poem, script, story or song.

ALL IN THE EYES

This is a great way to start an improvisation with direction from a partner. Students will discover the importance of the eye line and focus for communicating meaning and aiding performance.

1. Ask dancers to form pairs and face each other. Have them observe each other, taking a moment to become comfortable with their partners' gaze on them.

2. Ask one dancer to silently focus on one part of their partner's body. It doesn't matter where they direct their focus; it could be an arm, knee or hand, provided they give it their full attention.

3. Using an impulse to shift, they'll decide when that gaze will make their partner's body part move. This could be sudden or slow.

4. Have them look at another body part they can move in a similar fashion. They may continue this until they can almost control their partner with their eyes.

5. Instruct the partners to swap places.

6. Ask them to focus on a body part and try to move it using the direction of the gaze. If their eyes look up, their partner's arm would rise. The dancer can also move round the space whilst following their partner's directions.

7. Ask them to swap places again.

One dancer leads the other's actions with their eyes.

Teaching Tip

You may want to demonstrate how this works before you start step 3. It's also helpful to have calm, soft music playing in the background to help with this focus-based task.

Further Development

The partnership could develop into a duet, in which both dancers direct with their eyes and respond to the focus of the other's gaze.

MAKING MAPS

This is a good way to help dancers work cooperatively in pairs and think about how they can use space. You may want to cover stage directions prior to this task so they can describe where they are and where they intend to travel on stage.

   1. Ask students to form pairs and draw two different pathways on paper: one that's contained and one that's freer and uses more space.

   2. Have each dancer take one and bring it to life using three different ways to travel. They may walk, run, gallop, roll, crawl, hop, jump, spiral and so on. Have them choose whichever three they think best fit the journey or floor plan they've drawn.

   3. Ask them to swap pathways with their partners and, again, find three ways to travel that they think fit.

   4. Instruct them to come back together and show both pathways to their partners.

   5. Prompt them to decide how to put all four journeys together to present to the rest of the class.

Two dancers travel at different levels on a straight pathway.

Teaching Tip

The more interesting their drawn pathways are, the more complex their travelling will be. You can adapt this for different groups by having two ways of travelling or five ways that must include a swing action, for example.

Further Development

Dancers will have a rough plan of how a dance piece can travel through space. They can layer other ideas on this journey, perhaps including phrases they've created from other tasks. They could stop and move in unison or stop when they're far apart and move in canon.

FALLING THROUGH CENTRE

Dancers should be warm before exploring this task. They'll be creating a solo motif that involves 'falling through centre', so you may want to explain what 'place' and 'centre' mean in dance.

Place is where you are. You're in place. You can have your arms above you in high place or by your side in low place. The term is used in dance notation, such as Labanotation, to show where steps and gestures may happen. With steps, place can also mean 'on the spot'.

Centre can be your core, but it can also refer to an imaginary line that runs through the centre of your body, especially in ballet.

1. Ask dancers to select three to five body parts from the following list:

- Arm
- Shoulder
- Elbow
- Hand
- Hip
- Head
- Knee
- Nose

2. Ask each dancer to find a way to raise each body part as high as possible above them as if they're being pulled by an unknown force. This could be up to high place, for example.

3. Prompt them to improvise with reaching up as before, but now let each one fall through their centre to touch the floor. This would be the most direct pathway to the floor. It can be controlled at first. Have them think about the movement and taking the quickest path to the ground so they're giving in to gravity. This is purely an exploration, so encourage them to try each one several times until they come up with something interesting.

4. Instruct them to select the movements they considered most interesting and join them. They could also make two parts of their bodies rise and fall together or in canon.

5. Dancers can then share their explorations with a partner and ask them to set the timing and use of breath.

Dancers explore dropping the pelvis, hands and arms through place.

Teaching Tip

This task can work well if dancers have a chance to share with a partner for feedback, use a mirror to see how the movements look or have access to a camera to film and watch themselves. You could describe the floor as a magnet that pulls their actions down.

Further Development

This task is about finding the quickest route to the floor. Dancers could explore how to perform this at any moment within a known phrase, step pattern or jump. They could find the route using several sharp movements, like a knee into the floor or a shoulder followed by the rest of the body.

RECALL, REMEMBER AND MOVE ON

This creative task allows dancers to build a short duet together quickly. They must use and remember their first responses and build on them as quickly as possible in order to recall, remember and move on.

1. In pairs, dancers will create something they remember and can recall. They'll find a movement answer to each of these words: 'explore', 'recall', 'remember' and 'move on'. You could add a time frame to each one if needed. This is moment 1.

2. Ask them to explore defining the space round their partners using a circular arm movement. Each dancer could create a solo moment whilst their partner is still or moving, and they could take it in turns as many times as they'd like. They must quickly recall, remember and move on. This is moment 2.

3. Have dancers explore three continuous movements (e.g., turning, rolling or stepping) at different levels from their partners' so they complement each other. Again, they must recall, remember and move on. This is moment 3.

4. Ask them to face each other and perform a brief movement in unison. Again, they must recall, remember and move on. This is moment 4.

5. Explore movements that travel round in a small circular pathway together. They can travel anywhere in the space in any way. Again, they must recall, remember and move on. This is moment 5. They might want to take 10 seconds to recall moments 1, 2, 3, 4 and 5.

6. Have them discover a reach or stretch they can do in unison, but each partner should find a contrasting way to fall or drop out of it. Again, they must recall, remember and move on. This is moment 6.

7. Dancers should use the moments they've collected and join them in any order with transitions, if they recall them. The challenge is to see how much they've remembered and, more interestingly, why they recalled it. Transitions could include turns, going into and out of the floor, steps or anything that fits what they've created.

Two dancers recall a movement together that they can perform for moment 4.

Teaching Tip

Each duet could add to this list to use themselves, or they could create a longer list with the ideas being used by all duets.

Further Development

Pairs could share with others to receive feedback and learn each other's movements. These duets could be performed in unison or one at a time within a piece as dancers move on and off the stage, in any order they think is interesting to an audience.

AWARENESS

This task helps dancers be observant of each other and pre-empt what they might do next. They'll need to be warm and open to exploring new ideas.

1. Ask them to form pairs, find a place away from others and face each other.

2. Have them explore their awareness of each other so they can sense when their partners are going to move or stop, attempting to move at the same time with the same speed.

3. Here is a list of things for the dancers to explore:

- Can they run and stop at the same time? They can try this repeatedly in different pathways, with each one instigating the run.
- Is it possible to give away clues that they're preparing to jump?
- Can they walk and turn at the same time?
- Can they go into, along and out of the floor at the same time?
- Can they create a contact moment with each other at the same time? Could they each place a hand on each other's heads at the same time, for example?

4. Once they've explored a few of these ideas, ask them to create a short, structured improvisation in which they'll perform three known actions (e.g., travel, touch elbows and go into the floor together). They can choose three or more on their own.

5. Ask them to share with others and discuss how a structured improvisation adds uncertainty or another layer of meaning to dance.

Two dancers explore going into, along and out of the floor together.

Teaching Tip

Ask dancers to swap places and experience pairing with different people. They could stop and discuss the experiment and try things that aren't on the list.

Further Development

You could also try this task in smaller groups of three to four dancers or even a larger number of 8 to 10. The groups could create lists of things to explore or have one per dancer that they write and place in a hat for selection.

SPACE SWAPPING DUET

This is a duet task that requires students to create phrases on their own and teach them to their partners. They need to be warm.

1. Ask dancers to find partners and have a brief jog round the room together whilst trying to run and stop at the same time without talking.

2. Direct them to separate and perform two movements on the spot that they feel define the space for them. This could be a reaching arm gesture, a rond de jambe or something that happens on both middle and low levels.

3. Instruct them to join both actions so they move them into and out of the floor.

4. Ask dancers to explore and refine these two movements whilst travelling. They can turn, step, roll and use their limbs to stretch out as far as possible. They'll now have four movements.

5. Ask them to rejoin their partners and share these phrases with each other. Each pair will then have eight movements.

6. They can use these movements together in any order they think works. They can also change positions as if they're in the centre of two circles. Ask them to emphasise the movements so they travel round each other like satellites. They could also find a unison or canon moment together.

7. Dancers can also explore this whilst adding the running from step 1.

8. Ask each pair to share with another to receive feedback and provide them with something to perfect as they rehearse.

Chapter 3 – Solo and Duo Improvisations   63

Two dancers teach each other their low-level, space-defining movements.

Teaching Tip

Some dancers will understand step 6 with a clear vision of how these movements will fit together and be shared. You may use one of these pairs as an example to help inspire other dancers' choices.

Further Development

You could teach the entire class one pair's dance to have a whole group moment within a piece of choreography. You'd not only be able to see pairs but two groups of unison performing.

FALLING AND FAILING

This improvisation task explores trust and counterbalances in pairs. Dancers will need to be warm and aware of the safety considerations of working this way.

1. Ask them to find partners and, holding elbows, find a way to travel round the room with one dancer leading. They can swap places and explore being led with their eyes closed.

2. Either with current partners or new ones, dancers can explore what would happen if one of them fell asleep whilst standing. First, ask them to try with their eyes open so they can save themselves if their partners don't catch or support them. They can attempt to be soft by bending the knees so they slowly crumble rather than fall.

3. Ask them to hold one of their partners' hands and observe what happens if one of them slowly falls. Swap places. They could also explore standing side by side and facing each other.

4. Now that they've explored this, they can become more confident with the outcome.

5. Ask them to hold both hands with their partners and take turns falling one at a time or at the same time, but in real time.

6. They could explore falling on their partners, giving them their body weight slowly. They could start with just their heads, then perhaps they could try their whole bodies.

7. Can they find a way to join these explorations whilst travelling on a straight pathway, perhaps from upstage right to downstage left? They can walk, run or use any combination of travelling actions.

Dancers find a way out of their contact moment after exploring falling.

Teaching Tip

Dancers need to work with partners they trust, who will go through this process with them and respond quickly. You may have to swap some pairs to ensure this.

Further Development

You can also have a larger group hold hands and create a continuous line of one side falling and the other side coming out of the floor after they've fallen.

HELPING HANDS

This is a good improvisation task for developing partner work, trust and connection. Make sure students are warm and that they've been briefed on the safety considerations of contact work.

1. Ask each dancer to find a partner and go to one side of the room together.

2. Have them find three ways in which they can help their partner travel across the space. This could be to

- push or nudge them on their way,
- safely pull them by a body part (e.g., a hand would work well),
- pick them up and carry them in a variety of ways and
- verbally encourage them to move across the room.

3. Ask dancers to share their duet with the whole group and then swap partners so they each have a chance to help the other across the room.

4. Instruct them to explore sharing the help so they both help each other, alternating as they travel across the room. If the room isn't long enough, they can travel back to where they started together.

5. Have them find three moments they think work best and decide on three places in the stage space in which they'd be performed. Find a way of travelling between each chosen stage direction, together or apart, to create a sequence.

One dancer uses contact by holding another's arm to negotiate their journey through the space.

Teaching Tip

If dancers are brave and have trust in their partners, they'll produce some wonderful travelling duets that seem to bob, weave and curl through the space. You can stop them at any time if you think an injury may happen or if a pair did something interesting that could be shared.

Further Development

If the pairs can recall, set and rehearse their travelling actions, they can start to develop and manipulate them effectively. For example, they could incorporate two lifts, an action that goes into the floor and a unison moment.

DISRUPT THE AIR

This improvisation uses a clear theme to create ideas. Dancers will be working on their own and in pairs.

1. Ask them to find partners and see if they can run and dance round the room so fast they can feel the wind they're making.

2. Ask each dancer to create three still positions inspired by three of these wind-related words: whirlwind, breeze, crosswind, gale, blustery, twister, upwind and gust.

3. Ask them to join these positions by turning, going into the floor and performing a balance that suddenly explodes to create a short solo phrase.

4. Instruct them to learn their partners' phrases and join them so they can be performed in unison. Ask them to remember the words they originally used so their intentions are carried into this longer phrase.

5. Have the partners move round each other and try to disturb the air surrounding them. Remind them to consider the actions, speed and dynamics required to create a breeze their partners can feel.

6. Ask them to join the following: the running to create wind, the unison phrase made from wind-related words and the duet explorations that disturb the air.

Two dancers move round each other using dynamics to create a breeze.

Teaching Tip

When dancers link all these ideas, they can place them in any order or fragment them. There are no wrong movement answers.

Further Development

You could try this task again but in different group sizes or themes (e.g., fire, water and so on).

DRAWING WHILST SUPPORTED

This pairs task will require trust because dancers will be taking weight whilst moving. This will create a short phrase that could be used in a longer piece.

1. Ask them to form pairs in which each partner can support the other.

2. Direct them to explore a counterbalance so each partner pulls away from the other and takes their weight. They can start by facing each other, holding one opposite hand, bending their knees and slowly leaning away from each other. They could try holding each other's wrists to find a more stable position.

3. Ask dancers to explore different ways to move into this counterbalance (e.g., stepping, turning or reaching) with a slow, controlled dynamic.

4. Have them explore ways to come out of their counterbalance (e.g., lunging, turning or falling), again with control.

5. The pairs will now have ways into and out of the counterbalance that can be different from each other. Ask them to go over this so it has a fluid dynamic.

6. Ask each dancer to counterbalance with their partner and draw an arc, line, circle or angular line through space with their free arm. For example, they could draw a line in the surrounding space whilst being supported. They can do this together or one after another.

7. Add this all together: the transition into the counterbalance, the tracing of the arm and the transition out of the counterbalance.

8. Ask each pair to teach their moment to another. This will help them understand timing and actions because both pairs can now perform in unison.

One dancer is on another's back, giving their weight and gesturing above with their arm.

Teaching Tip

Sometimes dancers can be inspired by each other. If you find a pair that works well together, perhaps they can demonstrate for the rest of the group. In addition, when they share with others, they can direct and suggest improvements.

Further Development

Each pair could share with all the others and create a longer duet or piece from fragmented movements. They could also continue to explore these counterbalances but in groups of three. When two dancers counterbalance, the third can provide support. For example, they could take leaning dancers onto their backs.

TRAVELLING IN PAIRS

This task develops awareness of moving with a partner – knowing when you're moving in a similar or contrasting way. It encourages dancers to work in pairs, increases spatial awareness and raises heart rates.

1. Ask them to find partners and walk round the room, side by side, exploring as much space as they can in one minute. They must work together to remain side by side, travelling in any direction (avoiding collisions with other pairs). To increase focus and concentration, encourage them to do this silently (i.e., no talking).

2. Remind them that there must be no leader.

3. Once they've accomplished this at a walking pace, ask them to gradually increase their speed so they're running. Make sure they stay side by side even when they change direction on their chosen pathways.

4. Have them try alternating speeds from walking to running and back without directing each other. Challenge them to vary their speed from a slow walking pace to a fast run and observe.

5. They can now incorporate moments of stillness by stopping or pausing during their joint walk or run.

6. Ask them to change their visual focus by switching from each other to the surrounding space.

Two dancers, side by side, run without leading or directing.

Teaching Tip

Observe them and ask if they have advice to share on tuning into their partners' movements. To encourage them to travel in a range of directions (rather than simply circles), you can show them diagrams of interesting floor plans and pathways. Ask them how they think this could develop into a short beginning section of a dance piece and what music would add interest.

Further Development

They could also experiment with increasing the distance between partners (e.g., 1 or 2 metres or 3 to 6 feet). You could also try this exercise in groups of three.

LIGHTING LINE

This is a solo task, but it could be explored as a pair or small group. One person would be the dancer. The other would take on the role of a choreographer or lighting designer who suggests actions, makes final decisions and orders movements. It would bring the dancer's attention to the notion of playing with lighting states.

1. Ask each dancer to imagine they're standing behind a thin line of light that runs across the floor from stage right to stage left. The light should be about 10 centimeters (about 4 inches) wide. The area behind it is in darkness.

2. Ask each dancer behind the line to find a suitable position, perhaps slightly flexing the knee for balance. This could be parallel, a lunge or a fourth position in turnout.

3. Instruct them to reach into and out of this imagined light, exploring different ways to reach and move with both arms.

4. After their explorations, ask them to select three different ways and combine them with a slight rotation of their bodies between each one.

5. Have them use their feet to reach and explore into and out of this imagined light, finding different ways to do this with both legs (e.g., circling, throwing or pointing).

6. After their explorations, ask them to select three movements that worked well and combine them, again performing a slight rotation with their bodies between each one. They could also change their facing.

7. Ask dancers to join the reaching arm explorations with the legs. They could perform the arms first and then the legs or alternate. Ask them if they can vary the speed and quality of these actions. Could they make them more interesting?

8. Instruct them to explore with their arms and set two movements that can carve or slice through the light's edge, slowly and deliberately.

9. Have them add these slicing actions to the arm and leg reaching actions and share with partners, using music for timing and emphasis.

Chapter 3 – Solo and Duo Improvisations

A dancer reaches and pushes out into the imagined light with one hand.

Teaching Tip

Students will produce interesting results if they play with light in a dark setting because they can interact with it more effectively.

Further Development

Dancers could work with partners and add their sequences together to see what looks effective. They could pick and refine the movements that work to create a short section of a piece.

TRACING THROUGH SPACE

This is a simple yet effective solo task to help dancers think about spatial pathways parts of their bodies can create to generate interesting movements. Make sure they're warm and ready to create.

1. Ask dancers to pick three parts of their bodies (e.g., elbow, head and hand).

2. Instruct them to trace an outline with the first part after choosing a size, level, shape and plane. For example, they could make a small line with the elbow on a low level and vertical plane or a large circular movement outlining the head on a low level.

3. Have them trace another movement with the second body part but in contrast to the first. The contrast could be in size, level, plane or even speed. They could change where it's performed in the studio or which way their bodies are facing.

4. The third tracing can contrast or complement the other two.

5. Ask dancers to join these three actions to create a short phrase. Prompt them to consider how to transition from one action to another continuously.

6. In pairs, they could perform their phrases for each other whilst thinking about where the front is and the best viewing direction.

7. Ask them to find a way to join their two phrases to create a longer sequence.

Two dancers develop their own space-inspired phrases to create a duet.

Teaching Tips

Dancers could use their individual responses created in step 6 with a partner and discover how these phrases can complement each other when danced at the same time.

Further Development

Dancers could develop two phrases together. One would fit movements together as they interlock or fill the space round each other. The other would allow them to complement each other's actions. Instead of tracing the outline of a body part, they could write words or draw outlines of objects, people or even skylines.

SHIFTING SPACE

This improvisation gives dancers awareness of the space surrounding them and encourages an imaginative response through dynamics and visualisation. They'll initially work on their own but there's room for a duet or even small group work.

1. Ask them to find a space away from each other and imagine a giant screen with images, folders, maps and games in front of them. This will take up height and width.

2. Have them reach with one hand, select a folder and move it to a different place on the screen whilst moving an image into the trash with the other hand.

3. Ask them to move other imagined items round, varying the speed. For example, they could perform 15 movements in 15 seconds.

4. Instruct dancers to imagine the screen as an arc or large circle round them. The larger, the better. Have them move one item on a pathway round another to a new location. Encourage the use of levels and maintaining contact with that imagined item throughout the journey.

5. Ask them to swap hands and move as many things as possible, varying the speed, force, level, pathway and to move with intent so that the movements begin to have a purpose.

6. Direct them to find partners and describe their imagined screen shape and size to each other, then explore their partner's screen demonstrating the movements or types of movements they feel are most effective.

7. With their partners (as A and B), they can explore two ideas. They can swap at any time and decide if the imagined screen is flat or curved.

- The first idea is that A moves the items on the screen at a slow speed, and B moves them back from where they came. They can explore moving faster and see what happens. They may have to duck down or move round, over and under each other.

- The second is that when A is moving, B tries to move the folder to a different plane, perhaps using an interesting pathway.

8. After discussing what works best, dancers can now alternate what's moved where and shift the actions into a bigger space, perhaps even using the whole studio.

One dancer envisions a screen and pushes imagined items to the side.

Teaching Tips

They can discuss what the screen might contain in pairs before embarking on the solo task if they need inspiration or assurance that they're on the right track.

You could also discuss the word 'intent' and how that might change the dynamics and meaning of the movements. Is there a narrative attached to the movements that inform the dynamics?

Further Development

This could develop into quartets with two screens. Dancers could begin as duets and graduate to swapping their actions and reactions from screen to screen. They could use the same improvisations in number 7 but with two, three, four, five or even six Bs reacting.

EPIC JOURNEY

This is a good task to help dancers think about themes and imagined environments. They'll be running, so please ensure that the floor, footwear or bare feet aren't slippery.

1. Ask each dancer to draw their journey to school or any journey through a community on paper. They can add places and people they see on that journey.

2. Ask them to swap their documented journeys with partners and bring each other's journeys to life. They can travel in different ways (e.g., walk, run, gallop, roll or crawl).

3. They can also add actions to represent the people and things they encounter or observe on those journeys.

4. Ask them to share with each other. Did they learn anything interesting about each other's journeys?

5. Have them bring these journeys together however they'd like to make an interesting dance moment. They could both learn each other's or have separate moments that are different but come together at varying points. They may encounter moments in which they meet other dancers and create new interactions. Here are some ideas they could try:

- Stop and have a moment of joy – enjoy something. Make the movements as large as possible.
- Stop and have a moment of anxiety – think how this might affect the dynamics.
- Stop and be surprised to see each other – could they incorporate a jump, fall or breath?

Three dancers explore their own journeys across the dance space.

Teaching Tip

Dancers may struggle to document their journeys, especially if they feel they're not interesting enough. They're welcome to base these on reality or imagine another person's journey.

Further Development

Dancers could use these in a performance group to create an initial section that shows people travelling. They could also structure it with chance. For example, choreographer Merce Cunningham used chance-based structures, often with dice or other self-developed methods, numbering the options and letting random sequences set the order of a dance piece.

chapter

4

Group Improvisations

This chapter explores the movement responses dancers can generate in groups. By working with others, they can explore and discover new movement ideas. The tasks within aim to develop, challenge and refine creative responses and the feeling of working as a team that comes with making group decisions in the moment. Similarly, they'll help students become ensemble dancers with an awareness of themselves and others from moment to moment. Working as an ensemble dancer, or corps de ballet, takes observation, time, thought and skill.

WALK, STOP, SIT, LIE

This improvisation helps dancers working in groups build awareness of each other. It also introduces the idea of levels as a device for contrasting choreographic material.

1. Ask the whole group to walk, stop, sit and lie. Mix it up a bit. They can repeat several after each other and try to find a smooth transition into and out of each one.

2. Have them decide when they want to do each one and explore the results. You may need to add a rule requiring them to change after five seconds.

3. Ask them to repeat step 2 but in groups of four or five.

4. In their groups, have them perform the four actions without duplicating one. They must be observant, responsive and reactive.

5. To challenge them, ask them to add fluid and sharp transitions when changing from one action to another.

6. Keep the duplication rule, but every time they change, they have to be near a different dancer.

A group of dancers engages with the concept of moving at different levels.

Teaching Tip

If you ask a few groups to share, you can discuss what worked or what didn't to be sure they're making the most of the task.

Further Development

Dancers could play with moments of contact instead of stopping. They could add motifs and phrases they've created in other tasks to add meaning at any point. Further, they could create a short motif for each of the four actions they could attempt each time to add a layer of frustration or comedy. You could even add this as a structured improvisation section to any ensemble piece.

CONNECTION PERFECTION

This is a great task for creating a complex small-group moment that can fit within a whole dance piece. Dancers must be accustomed to working in small groups and making physical connections.

1. Ask them to form groups of three to five dancers. This can take place at the end of a warm-up game so they're ready to move.

2. Ask the groups to create two still shapes together. The rules for these shapes are:

- Both must be different so they contrast in some way (e.g., level or facing).
- Dancers must connect with each other. Both hands must make some connection with another dancer. It could be interesting if they form a knotted shape.

3. Ask them to find 8 to 12 small movements they can make to change from one shape to the other.

4. Give them time to remember these transitions.

5. Direct them to add dynamics to each movement, including rhythm. Dancers who need a challenge could add a different eye line for each movement, together or one at a time.

6. Guide them to use the connection they've made to aid each other into a third shape. They can push, pull or nudge another dancer into a movement. For example, they could push a shoulder down to take that dancer into the floor and into a roll.

Chapter 4 – Group Improvisations   87

Dancers create a still shape by connecting with each other.

Teaching Tip

Ask dancers to observe each other and discuss in small groups what they felt looked effective. Then have another go.

Further Development

Dancers can develop their ideas by making connections with different parts of their bodies. They could even try creating a meaning for each action from the theme of the choreography, which might change the dynamics and quality as well as the eye line of the dancers. They could also play with creating more than two shapes or develop travelling in between or alongside the complex shape shifting.

BATTLE LINES

This improvisation can create moments for use in a dance piece with small groups. Dancers must be warm and ready to work on their own and in groups.

1. Ask them to find a way of stepping round the room that's exaggerated or has an unusual speed, quality, size or dynamic.

2. Encourage them to explore ways of kicking in different directions between their stepping actions. The kicks could be forwards, sideways, backwards, low, on one knee, slow or with a jump. It's open to interpretation. Any kicks they demonstrate are appropriate if they're safe.

3. Direct dancers to travel using these two actions together. They could step round the room and kick when they want to, varying the actions each time.

4. Have them explore turning and varying the levels, speed and emphasis, as well as the directions they face and the body parts leading the turn.

5. Now that they've explored stepping, kicking and turning, instruct dancers to pick their most interesting actions and join them to make a travelling phrase on a straight line. Prompt them to visualise the phrase as a battle they're having with the space they're travelling through.

6. They can add any other actions they wish and use another kick or turn if it's different and travels the length or width of the space.

7. Ask them to join with another three to four dancers and share their travelling phrases.

8. In these groups, direct them into a line across the upstage or from upstage to downstage. This can be stage left or right so they have enough room to travel.

9. Dancers can decide when to perform their phrases – in turn or at the same time. They could try both.

Chapter 4 – Group Improvisations

Dancers kick whilst travelling on a straight pathway in a line.

Teaching Tip

Dancers may want to work in their small groups from the beginning and then separate and return to share ideas before placing them all together.

Further Development

If the groups can work out the phrase in retrograde, they can retrace their steps to where they started. They could also join with other groups and take turns dancing their phrases forwards as if meeting each other in battle.

STRUGGLE

This task will help groups of four to five dancers create a short section of a dance piece from one motif idea. They must be warm so they can safely create interesting responses.

1. Ask dancers to form groups of four to five.

2. Ask them to briefly step or turn away from their groups in order to create something original.

3. Prompt them to create their own solo motifs from these words:

- 'Struggle': They could visualise being trapped or caught in something and trying to break free. They could imagine they're mammals caught in plastic in the ocean, for example.
- 'Gasp' or 'breathe': A short, sharp breath can add a high point or drama to the motif. Perhaps they're under water and must quickly take another breath.
- 'Fall': Dancers could fall with their whole bodies, one body part or several parts.
- 'Outside forces': They can interpret this word in any way they think works within their motifs. They could move as if they're being pushed down, pulled up, moved sideways or saved from whatever was making them struggle.

4. Ask dancers to go back to their groups and share their phrases. They can help each other with timing and use dynamics to give their motifs a sense of flow. This could be called the 'solo phrase'.

5. Direct each dancer to choose one of their movements to teach the rest of the group so they can combine them to make a new phrase. They should make the movement happen on one count. This would be a sudden action in unison followed by three counts of stillness on a 4/4 bar. Music may help them perform the action on the first beat of the bar. To summarise, this phrase has a sharp movement, three counts of stillness, another sharp movement, more stillness and so on. This could be called the 'unison phrase'.

6. Ask them to set this to the music or counts and loop it so it's neverending. They can also decide on a formation. Standing in a line facing the audience can work well.

7. They've now created a solo phrase and unison phrase. They can perform the unison phrase in a loop, in which each dancer comes out to

Dancers in a line perform their struggle moments from the unison phrase, whilst one performs their solo phrase in contrast.

perform their solo phrase and then rejoins the unison phrase in the correct place. They could decide to use chance or come up with an order together.

8. Groups can share and perform for each other.

Teaching Tip

The sound score or music dancers choose will enhance their solo phrases, add dynamics and give clear counts to the unison phrase. You may need to give them ideas and feedback so they can create their own phrases with ease.

Further Development

Groups can develop both the unison and solo phrases so they travel round the stage space. Rather than being static and facing one direction in one formation, they can change where they are, where they're facing and what formation they're in.

BODY AS SET

This creative task helps dancers explore how using space and avoiding obstructions can force them to make decisions in the moment and challenge their improvisation skills. They're using their bodies to create a set design for other dancers to interact with.

1. Ask dancers to stand spread out. Divide the group into three by allocating every dancer a number one, two or three.

2. Inform them that, when their number is called, they have to find an interesting still shape to hold. This can be standing, kneeling or lying down, but they must be able to maintain it. Try this quickly by calling out 'one', 'two' and 'three' so they can find shapes that work for them.

3. Whilst a third of the group holds a position, the others will find ways to safely travel round the space. This could include avoiding, going round, moving over or travelling through these shapes. They could start by walking, but encourage them to explore new ways to travel.

4. Call out two numbers so there are more static dancers to interact with. As they go round, the moving dancers can also decide to copy any of the shapes, echoing the stillness in their movements.

5. In groups of four or five, have them take turns standing still whilst the others move. If they're in a group of five, three or four dancers would stay still whilst one or two would travel round or in and out as fast as possible by running, rolling and echoing.

6. Swap places. Discuss if there are any moments in which static performers could be used to swing round or help push the travelling performers on their journeys.

Dancers use their bodies as obstructions for others to navigate.

Teaching Tip

If you have music playing throughout this task, dancers will respond with more rhythmic ways of travelling. You could also provide a theme (e.g., flight, escape and pursuit).

Further Development

After step 6, groups can decide on a sequence in which each dancer moves round the others, but is pulled, pushed, nudged and manipulated on their journey.

BOB THE OBSTACLE

This is a great improvisation to help dancers think about responding in the moment and develop their awareness of space. They'll be travelling across the space, so please ensure that the floor, footwear or bare feet aren't slippery.

1. Ask students to move to one side of the room and form lines of four to five so they have room to travel.

2. Ask them to find a way to cross the room but with obstacles in their way. You can suggest obstacles for their interpretation. Start with a few simple suggestions to see how they use them:

- Navigate a lot of bags on the floor. This can easily be set up with actual bags to try at first.
- Avoid crowds of people walking towards you. This can also be easily set up with everyone walking towards one dancer before they try again on their own.
- Avoid animal traps.
- Criss-cross through lasers.
- Go through different sized puddles.
- Wade through treacle.
- Travel across slippery ice.

3. Once they begin to use their bodies creatively, ask them to team up with a partner and cross the obstacles again together, helping each other. Can they pull, push, lift and support each other across? Play different types of music and see what happens to their quality of movement.

4. Ask them to observe each other and discuss in small groups what they felt looked effective. Then have another go.

5. Ask them to reflect on what they found interesting, select what would work in a piece and join it to share with the group.

Chapter 4 – Group Improvisations   95

One dancer moves towards a 'crowd', preparing to travel through it.

Teaching Tip

If you revisit this task in a subsequent workshop, you may find that the movement reactions and ideas are more sophisticated.

Further Development

This notion of spatial awareness can apply to many other situations when creating movement material. Imagining spaces and objects can often bring new layers of meaning or dynamics to a dance piece.

LEAD, REFINE, REPEAT

This task helps dancers copy movements exactly, encouraging them to observe and learn how they can be refined in the moment.

1. This is a version of 'follow my leader', so there's only one leader at any time. So the leader doesn't have to think about where they're travelling, they can use one of these three floor plans:

- A straight line across the space
- A circle
- A square

2. Ask them to pick one dancer to lead the others in the floor plan. This dancer will make a spontaneous movement they don't have to consider. This could be several movements but nothing too long.

3. Have them repeat the movement as they travel, each time refining and improving it to provide a clear use of space, an understanding of the dynamics and a possible meaning so their completed floor plan is the best version it can be. Have all other dancers follow and note what's different each time, taking it into their own performances of the movement.

4. Direct them to swap places until they've all had a chance to lead and refine a movement.

A line of dancers copies the leader, who refines and repeats a movement.

Teaching Tip

Stop and observe some of the leaders to share any pointers you think are working for them.

Further Development

Groups that are capable of being challenged can take this task further. Dancers can split from the group as leaders and rejoin whenever they want. Doing this will create more than one group, but they'll refine on their own, move away and rejoin the group. If you add music, this could be a chance improvisation section in a performance piece.

QUIET LINKS

This improvisation task will help groups make moving shapes and consider the way they can move together. Dancers must be warm before doing this task.

1. Ask them to work in groups of four or five and create a still group position in which they're close together. They could hold hands with each other. They must be aware of making connections.

2. Direct them to find another shape that has at least one connection and discuss what was effective.

3. Have them take turns adding to the overall shape, one by one, so they're aware of what it looks like from the outside as the shape builds.

4. They can come out one by one and look at the group shape before adding themselves back in if they wish.

5. Instruct them to create a shape in which they're aware of each other but aren't touching. Can they still create an interesting group arrangement?

6. Encourage them to explore slowly moving together without touching, aware of where the others are. They may move into another interesting shape. Can they keep moving, each time creating a new one?

7. Ask them to try moving slowly as a group, but this time they can make and break these connections with each other. Connections could include reaching to a shoulder with a hand or a head touching an arm.

8. Perhaps they could move into and out of several connections to create a phrase or sequence they commit to memory.

9. Ask them to rehearse and share with another group.

Chapter 4 – Group Improvisations

Dancers are in proximity without making a physical link with each other.

Teaching Tip

Dancers don't have to pull each other into position; it's about the shapes that are made during the sequence.

Further Developments

If dancers are choreographing a group dance, they can add different speeds, dynamics, pauses and balances. They could also consider travelling through each other and making the shapes travel across the space.

SLOW GROUP

This is a task for small groups. It will encourage them to reflect, refine and evaluate as they create. Make sure they're warm and ready to move.

1. Ask dancers to form groups of four to five and explore travelling slowly together in one direction.

2. Direct them as they travel:

- Ask them to stay together.
- Have them step, turn and go into the floor without moving away from the group. Can they all move on different levels?
- Determine if they can do this as an improvisation whilst staying aware of each other and not talking.

3. Ask them to discuss what worked well and what they could do with it next. Is this a way to finish a piece of choreography?

4. Ask them to explore step 2 again after discussing ideas or refine the ideas they did explore.

5. Instruct them to select some of the moments they clearly remember from the slow travelling and create three to five still moments as if they're having a publicity photograph taken. They could take photographs to see what this moment of stillness would look like to an audience.

6. Prompt them to discuss whether they've selected an appropriate still moment or if any others are more interesting.

7. Ask the groups to join these three to five moments with a turn or by stepping to a new position. If they liked how they originally moved into the positions, they can find a small movement or head gesture they can perform once they're still.

8. Ask them what they'd like to do next. Is there another task that could come out of the slow travelling?

Chapter 4 – Group Improvisations

A group stays together whilst slowly travelling to help dancers be aware of each other.

Teaching Tip

This task is about handing over some responsibilities to the dancers so they can consider what's useful and the outcome they want.

Further Development

Dancers could start the process again, but instead of moving slowly as a group, they could move erratically or fast but still stay close together. As they watch other groups, they could attach a meaning to it. Why would a group travel and need to be close?

THE QUICK ONE

Dancers will create a group phrase using moments created on their own and with their groups. The idea is for them to challenge themselves to react to each step as quickly as possible.

1. In a small group of any size, ask dancers to come up with one dance action. This can be anything. They must reach a decision quickly. They must also demonstrate this action together.

2. On their own, they'll create a short phrase with five different actions. Allocate a short period of time for this. They could use the following:

- A reach up with one arm
- A lunge to the side
- A reach forwards with one arm with the impetus in the shoulder
- A ripple through the spine
- A circular arm gesture that stretches out as far as possible

3. Ask dancers to perform at least one of these on a low level and reorder them so their version is unique.

4. Direct them to rejoin their groups and see what the actions look like when they're performed together.

5. Ask them to add one or several formations to make it look interesting. They can move from each formation in any way they like.

6. They could also try moving as they perform. Although not everyone will move at the same time, they should move with the intention to create additional energy.

7. Instruct them to add the one action they chose in step 1 back into the group sequence anywhere they like, as long as they do it in unison.

Dancers rejoin each other to discover how their own phrases will work as an ensemble.

Teaching Tip

This is a quick task, so you might want to time each task as they go. You could have an alarm sound when the time is up.

Further Development

Dancers could create more movements on their own and add these to the list in step 2. They could also create more together, either separate or joined for step 1. They could then be used throughout the sequence in step 7.

MAKE AND BREAK

This improvisation task requires dancers to work in small groups with contact, so make sure they're warm and know the safety implications.

1. Ask dancers to form groups of five or six. Have each group create a still position in which they're close together. Each dancer must also have a connection with two others with any body part.

2. Ask them to try to move in this position. They should still have contact with two others throughout, but the challenge is to break and make connections as they travel. The travelling will be slow whilst they work this out and they can move on different levels.

3. In contrast to step 1, prompt them to explore moving slowly at first, staying aware of where other dancers are and attempting to break the connection. In other words, a dancer would move away from the group, move back in and make two different connections. They'll have to start by doing this one by one, perhaps numbering themselves. When they move away, they can walk, run or perform a known sequence before rejoining the group.

4. Once they've all explored moving away from the group several times, they can now play with forming new groups. If one dancer moves away from the group and makes a still shape, and another dancer joins and connects with them, the rest must move to this group and connect. If the solo dancer is not joined by another, they must rejoin the original group. Either group must still try to travel.

Dancers in a group make physical connections with each other before breaking and moving on.

Teaching Tip

Each group can take as long as they need with each step. You may find that a group will spend longer on the task that appeals more to them.

Further Development

This task could also be explored in pairs. The connection moments could develop into counterbalances, supporting moments and lifts, which then break away.

EN MASSE

This improvisation game is a bit like 'follow the leader', except everyone must anticipate the leader's direction. How complex and visually interesting it becomes depends on the group.

1. Ask dancers to follow a given leader round the room. You can add anything you think will make it more challenging. You could suggest different ways to travel (e.g., walk, gallop, fall, jump or roll).

2. Whilst you have one allocated leader, the other performers can get above, below or in front of them. Wherever they are, they must still perform the actions the leader performs.

3. If they get it wrong, they have to move quickly to somehow rejoin the group.

4. They don't have to travel to the same places, but they must always stay close, like a troop of monkeys or flock of birds.

5. You can shout 'repeat' at any time and the dancers have to repeat their last action.

6. You can also call out for another leader at any point.

Dancers follow a leader (who points to the camera) and try to pre-empt what they'll do next.

Teaching Tip

This is one of those tasks that only makes sense to dancers once they've explored and attempted it. You may want to separate the group and have half moving and the rest observing before swapping. They could discuss what worked well with the observers and how to relate to the leader to make it more effective.

Further Development

This could develop into a new warm-up, wherein dancers explore the space together using a selected sound score, characteristic and aim.

MAKING AN ENTRANCE

This group improvisation introduces the idea of being seen on stage – of having focus, energy and stage presence. What dynamics or focus do you have to employ to be viewed by an audience?

1. This improvisation could start as a game, in which everyone is at the edges of the space and must make their way in, through, across and out, back to where they started. Dancers can decide when they'll enter the space, but there must always be at least two away from the edges. They can also decide what they do, how they move and what meaning or intention is behind the movement.

2. They also must consider how they'll exit the space and decide if they do this without paying too much attention to whether they want an audience to focus on them.

3. Ask them to enter and exit, stay in a space or on the 'stage' for 16 counts and perform a sequence they can recall or an improvisation before returning to the edge. They must perform as if they want to be seen.

4. Ask them to form groups of three or four and explore ways to enter the performance space together. What ideas did they get from watching?

- They could all enter from one place or from different sides of the space.
- They could walk, run, crawl, roll or use a mix of these.
- They can also consider where the space they're travelling to is.

5. Prompt them to explore how they can make an exit as a group.

- They could all move together and exit in the same direction or scatter themselves.
- They could turn, walk, leap, roll or use a mix of these.
- They could also consider where the exit they're travelling to is.

6. Once they have an idea of how they'll enter and exit, they can decide or create something to perform together before they exit the stage.

7. Once each group has an entrance, a moment on the stage and an exit, they can all come back together in the space and perform these together. When they go is up to them. You may find that some groups overlap and some are on their own. You can try this several times or decide an order you think works.

Dancers create a still moment on the wall before making their entrance into the space.

Teaching Tip

Explain that they don't have to be too energetic as they enter because this is just an introduction to a possible dance piece. If you use high energy at the beginning of a piece, you must match this throughout the section. It's possible to do this, but perhaps not at the start of a piece. They may want to discuss this further.

Further Development

Ask dancers to suggest a score or musical piece they'd start a dance piece with. You could try this task again but use a different piece. For example, you could use the beginning of a different piece each time.

GRAFFITI

This is a warm-up to help students visualise the body in space and where it's travelled, using parts of it to carve a designed journey.

1. Ask them to form small groups of three to five and briefly discuss what they'd graffiti if they had a huge canvas. Would they choose a picture, a portrait or an image of peace? Would they choose something for people to enjoy or to make a statement? If they could use art to give them a voice, what would they want to say?

2. Prompt them to think about leaving a trace or painting the space with this selected image as they travel on their own. Encourage them to use different levels, planes, directions and spatial pathways, all with different body parts.

3. In their groups, have them take it in turns to follow one another. This is a bit like follow my leader, but instead of following their partner's actions, they'll move through the traces they've made with different body parts and react to them with movement.

4. Have them swap places and explore making the traces more complex to challenge their groups.

Dancers are aware of the trace that their gestures will leave behind whilst following a leader.

Teaching Tip

Ask pairs to demonstrate and discuss what looked effective and how they could apply that to their own choreographies.

Further Development

Dancers could bring images with them to the next workshop and discuss how they could be turned into movements as a group.

BE ORIGINAL

This improvisation requires students to explore movement ideas from the same task, but the challenge is to create something different from others. This will challenge them to be original and create complementary movement material.

1. Direct them into groups of five to six and into a formation in which they can see each other. On their own, they'll need to explore their own movements inspired by the provided words. They can be on any level or any plane. The challenge is to respond to them in movement differently from others in the group, especially because they can see them. Dancers will create a short motif using all three.

- Uncurl one arm.
- Ripple both arms out to second whilst in a lunge.
- Unfold one arm up and one to the side whilst in a slight plié position.

2. Prompt them to explore their movements in a line with their groups to observe whether they're similar and could complement each other. Set this as sequence 1.

3. Ask them to explore this sequence again and decide on counts for each action. Have them twist into and out of the positions, perhaps using a rotation of their spines and shoulders.

4. Once they've decided which movements work, ask them to explore these dynamics:

- Speeding up with an ongoing feel
- Slowing down as if dragging something
- Stopping for a small breath
- Melting, dropping or falling, perhaps to the floor

5. Place these new movements together in any order, repeating them with different facings. Add a lunge, a back bend and several turns. Set this as sequence 2.

6. Join both sequences in the group and, perhaps, film or use a mirror to see interesting movement relationships.

Dancers explore uncurling one arm at different levels.

Teaching Tip

Step 3 is about finding a way into the previously explored movement by engaging the rest of the torso. Dancers can share and direct each other to select what works effectively.

Further Development

Students could write their own lists of words or phrases to explore for step 1. They might also find another emphasis for step 3 (e.g., uncurl, ripple or drop). They could also replace the additions in step 4 (e.g., gallop, fall, rond de jambe).

chapter

5

Moving Beyond the Kinaesthetic: Using Physical and Aural Improvisation Tasks

This chapter explores how starting with elements of physical and aural settings can lead students to create interesting, well-thought-out and purposeful dance. The physical setting in dance includes costume, set, lighting and properties. This chapter introduces the use of objects, including a tennis ball, chalk, chairs, tables, a bench, paper and a water bottle. The aural setting includes music, sounds, words, natural or found sounds and silence.

TENNIS BALL

Type: Prop Task

This is a good warm-up game to get dancers warm and is also beneficial to new groups in a new space. They'll be running and dodging, so please ensure that the floor, footwear or bare feet aren't slippery. You will need a tennis ball or similar object.

1. Ask dancers to form a circle. You can use a tennis ball to start with or simply the group's imagination.

2. Place it in the centre of the circle and ask each dancer to take turns running in and tracing their initials in the air. The faster, the better if you have a large group.

3. If the group is well practiced in dance skills, you can ask for different planes and levels. If not, just getting them into the circle will help with confidence.

4. The last person in the circle stays with the ball. Have them decide how to pass it to anyone else in the circle. For example, they can throw, roll or make it trace a pathway, letter or spiral to the other person whilst they're holding it.

5. You could remove it and continue to explore different ways to pass energy across the circle or replace the ball with a different object.

One dancer writes their initials with a tennis ball in the middle of the circle.

Teaching Tip

A tennis ball works well, but you could repeat this idea several times at the beginning of a workshop or lesson with a different object each time. You could also vary the size and weight of the ball.

Further Development

You could introduce several different props to see how dancers pass them to each other. Dancers could also add sounds to the movement of the object travelling through the air.

ORBIT SWING

Type: Prop Task

This is a creative task for dancers to explore in pairs. They'll need string or rope and a heavy object, like a water bottle or pencil case, to attach to the string. If they use a water bottle, have them explore filling it with water or sand to make it heavy enough to swing well. Where possible, you could safely tie the object to a lighting grid and dangle it about 1 metre (3 feet) from the ground. Dancers could also hold it.

1. Ask them to form pairs, select an object (e.g., water bottle) and tie the string to it.

2. Have one hold the string and object high up in the air.

- Have them try the following actions:
  - Swing it in a circle.
  - Make the circle bigger and smaller.
  - Make the swinging as slow as possible.
  - Change the direction of its travel.
- The other partner will respond to the swinging object in these ways:
  - Duck underneath and find continuous smooth movements into and out of the floor whilst avoiding it.
  - Explore gestures that echo the swinging or reach towards the object and follow its swinging journey, circular or otherwise.
  - Stop the object with both hands as it swings and find a moment of stillness. Consider the shape the rest of the body is making in this moment of stillness.

3. Ask dancers to swap and explore interacting with and swinging the object.

4. They can now select the moments that work and join them to create a phrase. This will feel spontaneous because the direction and size of the swing may change depending on the height, weight and force used. They could also find a way to swap the person holding the object as part of the dance.

One dancer explores ways to swing a water bottle whilst the other reacts and interacts with it.

Teaching Tip

Pairs will need a lot of space so they don't bump into others. You can allow time for a discussion on what worked best before they swap in step 3. If one dancer is holding the swinging object, it can work better if the responding dancer explores low-level floorwork and middle-level actions.

Further Development

Those holding the rope could stand on a table or platform, adding height and distance to the explorations. They could also find a way to move round the room so the movement changes location. If you've hung the object from a sturdy lighting grid, you could try other objects. For example, you could hang a speaker that swings and throws sound in different directions or a bucket with a hole that allows sand or water to fall through.

FLIGHT PATH

Type: Prop Task

These tasks require dancers to explore using paper as a prop. You'll need any kind of A4 paper.

1. Ask dancers to form groups of five to six and have three sheets of A4 paper.

2. Ask each group to scrunch one piece into a ball and pass, throw, catch (on their own and to others in the group) and gesture with it, perhaps in large circles at different levels. What other interesting ideas can they come up with?

3. Determine whether they can join these ideas for an ongoing feel to create a possible improvised dance section. They may want to give each dancer a paper ball and have them kick, juggle and roll, with and without it.

4. Ask them to pick up another piece to make a paper aeroplane. Whilst they do this, they could investigate how the folds could be echoed in movement. They could pass it to another dancer to complete each fold. For example, they could fold an arm in, fold their body over or move into the floor whilst one dancer folds the paper.

5. Once they've made their paper plane, they can try safely launching it into the air. Whatever the plane does, they must copy in movement. If it dives straight into the floor, they'll need to find a way to echo this, perhaps by falling onto a shoulder. Make sure each dancer has a chance to throw the plane. Remind them that improvisation will take them travelling round the room as they follow its path.

6. On their own, have them select two or three walking, running, flying, diving, rolling or falling moments and refine them so they can be performed with ease and feelings of flow and breath. They can also place them together in any order and make them travel.

7. Dancers can return to their groups and decide on a flight path round the room, now without the paper planes. They can discuss covering this floor plan as a group but perform their own sequence from step 6.

Chapter 5 – Moving Beyond the Kinaesthetic: Using Physical and Aural Improvisation Tasks

Dancers use a paper plane to inspire movements.

Teaching Tip

You may need extra paper, because some students will want to improve their folded designs. You may also ask more interesting groups to share step 7 to inspire others.

Further Development

Can they think of another way to use the paper? Perhaps they could fold it into a fortune teller or a boat.

PEOPLE WATCHING

Type: Text Task

This is an improvisation for pairs to discover ways to move and speak. It could also work well as a warm-up to have them speak before they move.

1. Ask dancers to find partners and, with the rest of the group, create two lines in the centre of the room.

2. Direct them to face their partners and describe what they see (e.g., 'brown hair', 'an earring', 'two ears' or 'blue top').

3. Instruct them to take a step back and keep describing.

4. Have them step back again and try to be heard by their partners, even though they're both speaking at the same time.

5. Have them step back until at the edge of the room.

6. Ask them to take a step forwards and describe how they think they feel. Please note that this step is for more mature groups.

7. Ask them to continue stepping until they're close together again.

8. Encourage them to try stepping backwards using pure description and forwards using emotions. For example, they could take two steps back and one step forwards, but their partners could take three steps back.

9. Have them step again, adding movements to accompany the descriptions. These movements could be obvious or abstract, or they could be small gestures, large actions or a mix. The challenge here is to speak and move.

10. Prompt them to share these improvisations with the rest of the group and discuss the possible meanings of the distance, movement and text used.

Chapter 5 – Moving Beyond the Kinaesthetic: Using Physical and Aural Improvisation Tasks

Two lines of dancers describe each other and step back to encourage moving whilst speaking.

Teaching Tip

If you ask a few groups to share, you'll discover some interesting aspects you may want to help the others enhance.

Further Development

Dancers could select, refine and rehearse some of the actions and text moments they felt worked or conveyed a narrative. They could also explore using movements as reactions to the text their partners are speaking.

REPORTAGE

Type: Text Task

This improvisation task allows students to develop ways to speak and move simultaneously. They'll begin to explore how words can be used as a sound score for dance.

1. Ask dancers to form pairs. Have one describe what they want their partner to perform, whilst the other responds to their words in movement. This narrator can take the words literally or add their own spin. For example, if the mover ran round the room screaming, the narrator could run slowly on the spot, silently opening their mouth as if screaming.

Here's a list of starters to help this process:

- They were pulled into the floor by a shoulder and moved across it by an unknown force.
- They suddenly flinched and gasped, leaving an expression of sheer terror.
- They jumped for joy and spun round to see where the voice was coming from.

2. The narrator must also find a way to respond to the one interpreting their words. They might follow them, echo some of their movements or make them bigger. Ask them to swap roles.

3. Ask one dancer to move first and improvise round the space, perhaps to low-level music. Their partner will describe what they see. Ask them to swap roles.

Chapter 5 – Moving Beyond the Kinaesthetic: Using Physical and Aural Improvisation Tasks

Dancers use descriptions to direct their partners, who respond in movement.

Teaching Tip

Dancers may have to speak quickly with a good volume so their partners, and even the audience, can hear them. You may find that a large working group will be noisy. This could be a good thing so they can speak loudly without being too self-conscious. You may also split them into smaller groups so half of the group can observe.

Further Development

Students could, as a separate task, write up a description of a dance they'd like to see. They could even memorise the words before working with a partner.

SIMPLE COMMANDS

Type: Text Task

This improvisation is for pairs. It could develop out of any warm-up task and introduces the use of spoken text whilst moving.

1. Ask dancers to find partners and space away from others.

2. Explain that one is the narrator and the other the mover. The narrator will say various descriptive commands and the mover will respond using a combination of the following movements (e.g., push your knee with grace or pull your elbow with vigour):

Push	your elbow		grace
Pull	your knee		vigour
Circle	your head		concentration
Drop	your shoulder	WITH	care
Lift	your hand		determination
Drag	your ankle		strength
Swing	your ribs		flair

3. Have them attempt to say the text with the actions happening almost together, without leaving a gap, so they're constantly moving. They might repeat some of their partner's words but change the end word. The mover can react several times, exploring different responses.

4. Ask them to swap roles so they both get to explore their use of text and responses.

5. For a challenge, direct them to swap back again but react in opposition to the commands.

Chapter 5 – Moving Beyond the Kinaesthetic: Using Physical and Aural Improvisation Tasks

One dancer directs their partner to push their elbow with concentration.

Teaching Tip

Stop and observe some of the partners to see if they can share any pointers. Clever dancers can make this quite amusing.

Further Development

If dancers can use commands one after another, they can speak and move at the same time. They can add any other words they want to help their partners respond.

TEXT TENSES

Type: Text Task

This is a quick solo improvisation for students to explore the notion of moving whilst speaking. It gives them an opportunity to address an audience and explain what they're doing. You could discuss being original and creating their own unique movements before they start.

1. Ask dancers to find space away from others.

2. Have them make a short phrase out of these three words: walk, sit and roll. Ask them to create a phrase they feel will be different from any others. It doesn't mean they can't walk, but they should add a direction, rhythm or arm pattern to ensure its originality.

3. Once they've decided on these actions and how they fit together as a continuous phrase, prompt them to share with another dancer or small group for feedback. This is a chance to make sure it's something they can remember and that it's a complete phrase of movement.

4. Ask them to layer this text over the actions:

- I'm going to walk. I'm walking. I walked.
- I'm going to sit. I'm sitting. I sat.
- I'm going to roll. I'm rolling. I rolled.

5. The challenge is to keep moving so they need to say the text at the right point in the phrase. They can share with other dancers.

6. Discuss what's effective and what they could add into the phrase to help it be continuous. Discuss where they need to direct the text. Is it out to the audience? Could it be to a partner? They could explore both.

One dancer describes and performs walking actions.

Teaching Tip

Keep it simple at first so the simultaneous speaking and moving are possible. Once dancers can do this, they can play with all the body actions, perhaps writing a few down first.

Further Development

Dancers can make their own phrases using any other words but should layer the text on top. They can play with it by adding meanings and, perhaps, humour. For example, they could say, 'I was going to turn, but instead I decided to fall to the floor to add drama to the fact that my partner touched my arm. Whilst on the floor, I'm going to spin. I'm spinning and now I'm dizzy. I'll now return to standing. I'm standing. I'm standing quite still but not that still, because my hand is waving'.

USING WORDS

Type: Text Task

The written language can be a powerful influence in inspiring the creation of dance. Even working from a list of words and highlighting the verbs can help, because they suggest actions that can generate movement ideas. The most successful texts are poems or monologues (e.g., *Hamlet*'s 'To be, or not to be' soliloquy).

1. Ask dancers to select a document or book containing words. These could be things like plays, poems, the news, nonfiction, fiction or any other written word articles.

2. Prompt them to read the text aloud and listen carefully to the language. It may contain a rhythm, alliteration, rhyme and so on.

3. Have them begin to move to the rhythm of the words, perhaps by placing the rhythm in just one part of the body (e.g., leg or shoulder). As they move, they could shift the emphasis of the rhythm into another body part (e.g., arm or hip).

4. In pairs, ask them to read the text, make a list of images that come to mind and create still shapes and positions that could be joined with transitions.

5. Have them read the text again and highlight the most meaningful words. Prompt them to describe the quality of these words in movement terms. In other words, do they suggest moving sharply, quickly, slowly, fluidly or low to the ground?

6. Dancers will have collected many ideas they could initially set as motifs to develop.

Chapter 5 – Moving Beyond the Kinaesthetic: Using Physical and Aural Improvisation Tasks

Two dancers hold books and interpret the text into movement.

Teaching Tip

Dancers may engage with all of these ideas, but if they are only inspired by one, it could be that the written words, script or book they have selected is limiting them or that they are inspired by just one idea and would enjoy developing this. If dancers are struggling to engage, maybe they can be encouraged to bring in a favourite comic or magazine. They may also find that working in small groups generates ideas they can explore together as they could all select a different way to use the words. As soon as you see them moving and responding, ask them to select and refine the movements to create a motif.

Further Development

You could ask half the group to observe the other as they share their ideas. Prompt them to discuss possible meanings these moments could have and which words they may have used. They could also share in pairs and, perhaps, help choreograph one another.

WORD SEARCH

Type: Text Task

This is a great task to help dancers think about their dance language. They'll consider how it can be interpreted to challenge the meaning of movement and how detailed a description must be to become movement.

1. Ask them to form pairs, read the following description of a dance duet moment and interpret it together to make it movement. They can add their own interpretations, timings, rhythms and dynamics. This will be sequence 1.

Two dancers face each other. One grabs the wrists of the other, pulls one arm back and pushes the other forwards, making their shoulders take a sudden movement. One dancer pulls the other under one arm so they turn. With one dancer again holding the other's wrists, they gallop and repeat the sudden accented shoulder movement. They repeat this action. Both let go and bring their arms down in front of each other and out high to the sides. Still facing each other, they gallop, one forwards and one backwards. Looking at each other, they circle each other, isolating their shoulders in a rhythmic way.

2. Ask them to add several movements in keeping with what they've created and write them down. This will be sequence 2.

3. Ask each pair to pass their description to another to interpret, again using these words to create movement to add to the duet. This will be sequence 3.

4. Direct them to join the three sequences in any order.

5. Encourage them to share their full version with another pair or perform for the whole group. Discuss what the meanings, intentions, themes, characters, emotions or narratives could be and how a different use of dynamics could complement or enhance them in rehearsal.

Chapter 5 – Moving Beyond the Kinaesthetic: Using Physical and Aural Improvisation Tasks

Two dancers interpret the given text in their own ways.

Teaching Tip

There's no wrong or right way for dancers to turn these words into movements. What they create may be very different, but if they're engaged and work well together, it wouldn't matter if they added new ideas.

Further Development

In the next session, dancers could explore how different music can also layer on different meaning. They could perform their duets to three different pieces of music.

They could research and find a piece of dance they enjoyed watching and write up a short part of it, describing what they've seen from moment to moment. They could bring these in to be interpreted in pairs or by the whole group.

SETTING A ROUTE

Type: Set Task

This task requires a set – a structure or frame. You could create your own structure in the middle of the room with an interesting use of tables, chairs or even physical education equipment. You could use other people in set positions. You'll need to set clear boundaries in terms of safety considerations to ensure that there are no injuries.

1. Ask all dancers to stand round the set, chairs or frame, about 2 metres (6 feet) away.

2. Have one make a fluid route through this set, deciding what this route is and, perhaps, travelling over, under, round, across and through. They'll also improvise the movements that work best as they perform. When they step out on the structure, they'll tag another dancer to start their journey.

3. Make sure all dancers have had a first journey or encounter with the structure.

4. At some point, you can replace the tagging so more and more dancers decide themselves when to cross. You might have a few on their journeys at the same time.

5. Encourage them to explore copying, following or chasing each other. Eventually, you can set a minimum and maximum number of dancers (e.g., between three and five).

6. It then becomes the whole group's responsibility to maintain those numbers, with people going in and out as they wish.

Teaching Tip

This improvisation game uses a set and can be played repeatedly with the same or different structure. It could also produce some choreographically interesting movement material and interactions. Students may want to write their ideas in a logbook or record them on video.

Further Development

Dancers could try this task whilst making physical contact with each other at different points on the journey. Have them form pairs and suggest how this might work. See if they can travel slowly across the structure together by pulling, pushing, taking weight, nudging, holding and so on. You could also take the set away, but ask them to use the same movements or, at least, a close version of them.

CHALK IT UP

Type: Set Task

Dancers will need chalk for this task because it requires them to design a possible floor set they can interact with. This task could be performed in a dance studio where you can clean the chalk easily or outside. If you're not able to use chalk, you can use string, wool or rope.

1. Ask them to find partners and use chalk to mark a space on the floor to use as a base. This could be any shape and size.

2. With their partners, have them help each other explore this space, including the floor, middle and high levels.

3. Encourage them to add an escape passage to their defined space so they can leave. Can they create a movement to perform as they exit?

4. Once dancers are out of their base, ask them to observe where they are and find a quick way to travel back in.

5. Ask them to show another group their findings and discuss what was effective.

6. If you have the space, ask them to form small groups and create chalk designs on the floor they can interact with. They could start with a version of hopscotch and be as creative as possible, perhaps even writing what movements should be performed and where. It could almost become a piece of dance notation.

7. Make sure groups have an opportunity to dance their way through their own creation before sharing it and exploring others.

Three dancers interact with a small piece of string defining the space.

Teaching Tip

If dancers have an opportunity to share part way through step 6, they'll start to develop more creative ideas.

Further Development

Ask students to find three ways to climb over an imagined obstruction. They could use each other to lift, support or counterbalance. They could also use chalk pens to create a vertical design on a mirror.

PARK BENCH
Type: Set Task

This is a great improvisation task if you want to start moving outside in the school playground or local park or if you have a bench you can use in your dance space. It works well for environmental, site specific and dance for camera pieces. Make sure dancers are warm and ready to create.

1. Ask them to run round the bench and count, in seconds, how long it takes.

2. Encourage them to explore placing their hands on the bench, hopping to see if it supports weight and how high they can hop. Maybe they can perform an arabesque.

3. Prompt them to find ways to sit on it at different points, for different lengths of time and with interesting ways to move into and out of sitting. This could be turning, using the bench to take their weight or turning under an arm.

4. Direct them to form pairs and improvise on the bench for one minute using these three actions: hopping or pushing off, travelling round and sitting on the bench.

5. If you have only one bench and a big group, time the groups and swap quickly, but make sure everyone watches each other.

6. Have them try another minute, but this time make the transitions more important than the actions themselves.

7. Ask them to create a simple phrase that travels from one side of the bench to the other and even round it. It could be about a journey that isn't easy and takes effort. This could be a physical journey on which they must push themselves along to advance. Could it have another meaning? What story do they think this sequence could tell? What actions, jumps, turns or balances are effective? How would stillness affect it? What if they watch or ignore each other?

Teaching Tip

Dancers could watch and observe as research. As a choreographer, you'll often be involved in research. You may read about something to make more sense of it, watch performances and films or interview people.

To research a site you want to perform in, it's a good idea to learn about its history as well as how and why was it made. Even better, you could watch and make notes, a video or a sketch of what other people do in that site.

With the bench, you could discover the following:

- How do people approach it?
- How do they sit on it?
- How do they get off it?
- Is there another way they interact with it?
- How do they pass it?

Dancers could use these observations to create their own short phrase to add to the group section they've created.

Further Development

Each pair could try combining their sequences with another's to see what looks effective. Could they push and pull each other onto and off the bench? They could pick and refine the movements that work to create a short section of a piece.

RHYTHM CONNECTION

Type: Music Task

This is a good game to get dancers warm and is beneficial to new groups in a new space. They'll be running, so please ensure that the floor, footwear or bare feet aren't slippery.

Using any 4/4 120 beats per minute track

1. Ask them to run round the room in their own floor pattern to music with a clear rhythm.

2. Direct them to run for eight counts, stop and clap their hands for eight counts. If clapping seems too easy, they could try another way to make a clapping sound with their hands on their body (e.g., thighs, shoulders, knees, arms and so on).

3. Encourage them to try four runs and four claps, then two runs and two claps and finally one run and one clap. Have them repeat and attempt to perform in different directions.

4. Ask them to try eight runs and eight claps, this time clapping hands with a partner. They must find a partner quickly at the end of eight runs. Again, they can create a more complicated way to slap and clap.

5. Again, ask them to try four, two and one.

6. Have them make eight runs, stop and find a partner and explore a phrase that uses hand claps. This could include clapping hands with their partners, clapping their own hands or one hand clapping each other's at a time. This will give them a combination.

7. Once they've created it, ask them to run round the room for eight counts to find each other and clap their own eight-count combinations.

Dancers explore rhythmic patterns together.

Teaching Tip

You can make this as complicated as you'd like, depending on the group. You could mix it up so they count up with the runs and down with the claps. They could run eight and clap one, run seven and clap two and so on. You could also let them decide when they run or travel and when they stop and clap.

Further Development

If they perfect and teach each other their phrases, this can develop into a long, complicated sequence. They could add travelling moments in between and change formation.

JUST THE MUSIC

Type: Music Task

This is a good warm-up to get students listening to music and seeing how another person is inspired to move. Find a piece of music you think your group would enjoy.

1. Ask dancers to form pairs.

2. Encourage them to move to the music. If they struggle, guide them to consider taking steps at different speeds in different directions.

3. Have them try following a partner as they move to the music. Ask them to mirror the movements, paying particular attention to what they do with their arms, hands and head.

4. They could try the opposite or even perform movements independently before returning to the mirroring.

5. Make sure they have time to watch other pairs move and dance. Observation is an important part of understanding what engages a dancer when movement and music work together.

6. This is a great way to learn from your peers. Make sure they swap.

Pairs of dancers follow or mirror each other's reactions to music.

Teaching Tip

You can number each pair and ask certain numbers to be still whilst others continue moving. This will give them all a chance to observe each other, gain new ideas and feel like they're part of the dance, even in a still position. Some dancers will come up with obvious movements, but if they're engaged and moving, they'll start to challenge themselves once they've observed the others.

Further Development

Once they've begun to trust that their partners will move in a way they can copy successfully, you could encourage them to move round the room. The notion of having some dancers in stillness may also be effective, and you could structure an introduction section to a dance piece.

FIND THE PHRASING
Type: Music Task

This is a good improvisation task to help find phrasing within a piece of music. Music and dance often share common structures, including phrasing.

1. Ask students what they think phrasing is. Allow them to listen to a piece of music and discuss what they hear.

2. Explain that musical phrasing is the way music is organised within measures. Where are the syncopations? Where are the cadences? Where are the accents? Choreographic phrasing is similar; it's how movements are organised with a beginning, middle, end and high point. A phrase in dance is the smallest unit of form.

3. Play a piece of music and ask them to see if they can walk, run, gallop and stop when they think it matches the music.

4. Instruct them to plot the notes of the music in the air with different body parts as if they're the semibreve (whole note), minim (half note), crotchet (quarter note) and quaver (eighth note).

5. Ask dancers to create a phrase of movement to a phrase of music after listening carefully. You could also create one for them. Perhaps you can discuss which moments in the score sound like turning, travelling or falling.

6. If they're creating their own, they could start by using their arms as if conducting the music and steps that accent notes, rhythms or sounds.

7. Ask them to use high points so they've considered where the music has more emphasis. The following are ways to create and enhance movements:

- Breathe in, especially on jumps.
- Suspend into falls using breath.
- Make the movement bigger, stronger or faster.

8. They might discover other ways to create phrases that hold the audience's attention as they dance.

9. Ask them to watch and help each other rehearse their phrases.

One dancer interprets a musical score using the notes to inspire movement reactions.

Teaching Tip

Having an interesting selection of music would be helpful. Here are a few suggestions to research with your dancers: Max Richter, Ólafur Arnalds, Nils Frahm, Hauschka, Ludovico Einaudi, Hildur Guðnadóttir, Nitin Sawhney, Sigur Rós, Jóhann Jóhannsson and Air.

Further Development

You may find that a visual aid, such as a written score, would help them see the notes, which may inspire their movements.

PLAYING YOUR PART

Type: Music Task

This is a music-inspired task, so make sure you've used music in your warm-up before you embark on this idea. Dancers will need a paper, a pen and a selection of music for this task.

1. Ask them to form groups of three to four and select a piece of music to listen to. They can lie down or get comfortable whilst listening.

2. Have them try and work out at least four instruments. They can discuss what they hear and when. They need to select one for themselves and listen to the music again.

3. Ask them to draw what they hear as lines, dashes, dots, marks or a graph – anything they feel represents their selected instrument.

4. On their own, have them interpret and turn their drawings into movements. They could associate the different marks with body actions. For example, a dot could be a jump and a line could be a way of travelling. A line could also be a pathway through the space. They can also take this path with a body part.

5. Ask them to rehearse with the music on their own.

6. Once they've completed their interpretation of an instrument, they could perform it in their groups to see what happens. They need to be aware of each other and avoid collisions.

7. Dancers can now begin to step outside the action one at a time and direct how these solos can fit together to become a group section.

Three dancers perform their movement reactions together whilst avoiding collisions.

Teaching Tip

There's no wrong way to do this. Some dancers may produce something small, perhaps on the spot, whilst others may make something larger moving through the space. Once they place these together, they can discover what's visually interesting. Sharing ideas at any point will aid the process. Some may be able to dance just hearing the music without having to use the drawn interpretations.

Further Development

This task also works well in pairs or even large groups, wherein dancers are almost a dance orchestra.

NARRATIVE IN MUSIC
Type: Music Task

For this task, students will need to find partners and listen to previously selected pieces of music together.

Ask them to think about what narrative, story or event the music may communicate to them. They can write this down or draw a visual interpretation. Once they have an idea, have them select several of the following to try to turn into dance:

Improvise in pairs: They can explore following partners as they move to the selected music. When they mirror their movements, remind them to pay particular attention to what they do with their arms, hands and head. They could try the opposite or even perform movements independently before returning to the mirroring actions. Make sure they swap.

Create a floor sequence in pairs: Pairs can explore movements on the floor that use rolling, taking their weight on just their arms and using their abdominals to sit up and hold positions. Remind them to perform these movements as fluidly as possible and add moments of suspension to create high points. They could discuss with their partners what looks effective and create movement together and apart to challenge themselves. Remind them that floor work can add a great contrast to their duet choreography.

Balance work: They could create five balances with their partners that use a give and take of weight. These could be counterbalances or lifts. Discover if they can get into and out of these quickly to create a feeling of high energy and risk. They may want to do this in threes so one person can always act as an outside observer and safety officer. They might stop their partners in a balance and let them lean on them whilst pulling them into a lift. Remind them that contact work can add meaning to their duet choreography.

Improvisation in pairs: Ask dancers to imagine that a huge hand is controlling their every move as they travel across the space. In these pairs, one dancer could be the hand making the suggested gestures: pushing, nudging, flicking and squeezing. The other dancer could respond by falling, jumping and so on. Ask them to swap and discuss what they think worked.

Action words: If the musical piece they've selected has lyrics, they could highlight all the action words (e.g., roll, fall and grab). They can then create their own version of these as movements and join them with transitions to create another short sequence.

A pair improvises to music so one moves as if controlling the other.

Teaching Tip

Dancers can also use visual inspiration. If they wanted to base a dance on an event or story, they could search for photographs or illustrations. Make sure they have time to observe each other, because observation is an important part of understanding what engages a dancer when movement and music work together. This is a great way for them to learn from their peers.

Further Development

Pairs could swap their music with another and work together to choreograph a dance to the entire piece of music.

chapter 6

Developing Improvisations

This chapter encourages dancers to use the movements, phrases and sequences created in previous tasks to play with development and structuring to manipulate the movement material. They can also develop ideas using existing material and repertoire.

YOUR RESEARCH TASK

Research is the initial part of the creative process for most choreographers. It's important because it helps underpin ideas, clarify intentions and justify decisions. It can also clarify why a choreographer wants to create a work, who the target audience is and what they may take from the experience.

Dancers explore ways to develop movements for 'love and connection'.

Step 1: Research Question

Choreographers may ask themselves questions like academic researchers or scientists. They may not be answerable, but they can give focus to a choreographic project. An example research question could be: Is it possible to create a full-length ballet for a modern audience with modern, real-world themes and concerns whilst maintaining the integrity of the original narrative?

Read through the following paragraphs and select one of the imaginary starting points. Write a research question you think is useful.

This piece was inspired by the concept of war – an event during which young and old men went and then disappeared. It uses the emotions, memories and themes in the poem 'In Flanders Fields' by John McCrae and several love letters written by soldiers to their loved ones.

It involves research into the narrative outline, musical score and characters of the original classical ballet, *Swan Lake*. It also includes other elements that present it through the lens of modern social and economic imbalances. It uses parts of the original score but aims to bring it into the 21st century.

This piece was inspired by the narrative, storyline and dramatic arc in Dario Fo's play, *Accidental Death of an Anarchist*. It also draws on the themes of insanity, exclusion, isolation, free expression and insomnia in *One Flew Over the Cuckoo's Nest* by Ken Kesey and *Fight Club* by Chuck Palahniuk.

This piece is inspired by the music of Yusuf Islam, also known as Cat Stevens. It was assembled from 12 of his songs, which share a narrative arc about the journey of a foundling from his birth to his final discovery and meetings with his father. The songs are: 'Sad Lisa', 'Where Do the Children Play?', a reworked version of 'Your Mother', 'The Wind', 'On the Road to Find Out', 'Old School Yard', 'Can't Keep It in', 'How Can I Tell You' and a reworked version of 'Father and Son'.

Step 2: Your Research Challenge

When doing research, you can also read material adjacent to the original theme or idea. You could collect many relevant or interesting pieces of information.

Research can also include the following:

- Reading adjacent to a theme or idea, looking into the meanings of words and finding quotes
- Finding other artists or pieces of art, dance, music, literature or theatre that have a similar theme or narrative
- Discovering artifacts and records from the same place, time or event

Following are three themes that provide great starting places for research and the early creative process. Pick one theme and three research tasks from the following list.

Research Tasks	Theme 1: Love and connections	Theme 2: Being an outsider and belonging	Theme 3: Life and death
Look up the meaning of the theme's words and use a thesaurus to help find many alternatives.			
Locate a quotation you find interesting from this theme. This is the repetition of a sentence, phrase or passage from speech or text that someone has said or written.			
Discover another piece of art (e.g., poem, music, film, book, dance, painting or photograph) that uses or starts with the same theme.			
Find an artifact, letter, news report or photograph that interests you about this theme.			
Learn about another dance piece that may have used this theme, even if in just one section.			

Step 3

Use the three things you've discovered about your selected theme to answer these questions:

1. What does this research help you understand about the theme?

2. What ideas can you use in your dance piece?

3. Do you need to do more research? What research will you do next?

Teaching Tip

Students may find it beneficial to work in pairs or small groups on these tasks. Encourage discussion and provide an opportunity to present findings to others. This will help clarify what's important and interesting as well as their next creative steps.

DEVELOPING PHYSICAL SKILLS

In addition to creativity, you'll want to encourage the development of physical skills. If students know what these are, they can take ownership of developing them in workshops, classes and rehearsals. One of the best ways to memorise a list of terms is to use a mnemonic device, like an acronym composed of letter prompts. For example, the following word may help students recall the physical skills used in dance. Following the word are three starter ideas to help reinforce it.

The Physical Skills Mnemonic: ICECAPS FABS

- **I**solation
- **C**ontrol
- **E**xtension
- **C**oordination
- **A**lignment
- **P**osture
- **S**trength
- **F**lexibility
- **A**gility
- **B**alance
- **S**tamina

Dancers in pairs create a warm-up using ICECAPS FABS.

Starter idea 1: In teams, dancers could have a Post-it note with each letter of ICECAPS FABS written on it. They must write the words associated with it and, in a relay with their team, run to the other end of the room and stick the Post-it onto the wall. Winners receive a point and then one for each correct answer.

Starter idea 2: Split the class into three groups. Give each group these letters: 'ICE', 'CAPS' and 'FABS'. As a group, they must remember the physical skills and devise a warm-up that would develop them as a dancer. They can set this to the music of their choice. Each group will then present their warm-up exercises or sequence to the rest of the group.

Starter idea 3: Dancers could create a short dance with a movement for each physical skill. They can, again, use ICECAPS FABS to remember the terms, but their sequence doesn't have to be in this order. They can choose their own music and share with the rest of the group.

DEVICES SURPRISES

Choreographic devices manipulate movement material and are often used to develop motifs for solo dancers. Manipulating is a way of developing or reusing movement in a new way whilst keeping some of its original essence. There are other devices for working in groups, such as unison, canon, contrast and counterpoint, but I will first list the devices that are most used when developing dance.

- **R**epetition
- **R**etrograde
- **C**hange of levels
- **C**hange of planes
- **I**nstrumentation
- **E**mbellishment
- **C**hange of quality
- **C**hange of force
- **C**hange of rhythm
- **T**iming and speed
- **I**ncorporation
- **I**nversion
- **S**taging
- **F**acing
- **F**ragmentation
- **A**ccumulation
- **B**ackground

A dancer develops movement material using BEAT.

Following is another word and three creative ideas to help with recall.

FABRICATES

Facing or fragmentation
Accumulation
Background
Repetition or retrograde
Incorporation, inversion or instrumentation
Change of quality, force, rhythm, levels or planes
Accumulation
Timing
Embellishment
Staging

Creative idea 1: After warming up and teaching the same motif or short phrase to the whole class, allocate one device to each dancer. This could be verbally, without the others hearing or on paper. Then, assign a short amount of time to develop it using just this given device. Each dancer will go round the room and perform their developed version to another, who will guess what device has been used. Continue until all dancers have guessed each other's devices. You could also have each one dance in turn so the whole group can deduce. Encourage discussion here, too, because they'll come up with great ideas that can be used again.

Creative idea 2: You could use smaller words to help dancers select several devices for manipulating a motif or phrase. Following are a few suggestions. Once dancers are warm or have learnt a short phrase, they could manipulate and develop it using these or their own words:

CRAFT
Change of quality, force or rhythm
Repetition or retrograde
Accumulation
Facing or fragmentation
Timing

BEAT
Background
Embellishment
Accumulation
Timing

STAR
Staging
Timing
Accumulation
Repetition or retrograde

CREATE
Change of levels or planes
Repetition/retrograde
Embellishment
Accumulation
Timing
Embellishment

Creative idea 3: In pairs, have them recall as many devices as they can and then face each other. Ask one to make a movement and the other to respond by developing it. This might mean repetition or making it fall to the floor and changing the level. Get them to swap and take it in turns to dance.

BACKGROUND

Dancers can use a range of devices to develop any movements, phrases or ideas along with one known as 'background'. This is where an action is performed whilst the rest of the body is doing something else. For example, when the torso and arms are moving, the rest of the body could be lunging, stepping or travelling. Dancers will need a phrase of movement to develop.

1. In pairs, ask them to select two movements from their chosen phrase. It will work best if this is something they perform with the arms or upper body.

2. Ask them to share ideas and work together to find a way to travel whilst performing the first movement or small phrase. This could be walking, running, galloping or rolling, as long as it's in keeping with their original theme or idea. They could call this travel 1.

3. Have dancers do the same with a second movement or small phrase they've selected but with a different way to travel. They could call this travel 2.

4. Ask them to join travel 1 and travel 2 with a moment of stillness between them. They'd have a beat where they just stop and find stillness before travelling again. Then, dancers will need to create an impulse to take them into the travelling.

5. Together, they need to decide where on stage they'll finish and where they'll make their entrance from off stage.

A group of dancers use a different background to the same action of having one arm extended high.

Teaching Tip

Please note that they can adapt the entrances and exits in whichever way fits with their theme or if their duets become part of a larger ensemble dance.

Further Development

Dancers could layer on the use of focus as they travel. They could look up, down, at each other, forwards, towards the audience, left or right. They could also highlight the impulse action after the stillness with the use of breath.

PRACTICE AND EMPHASIS

This task requires dancers to take on the role and responsibilities of being dancers. One of the things a dancer must do, often independently, is make sure they know the movement material and all the correct performance skills, such as focus, musicality, timing and dynamics to enhance the movement meaning. Rehearsal notes are often given by choreographers and directors to explore corrections and ways to improve performance and the overall piece. Dancers will need a phrase or sequence they've created in previous tasks.

1. Ask them to find partners, go over the movements they can recall from their chosen phrase and help each other remember and rehearse them, dancing in unison.

2. Scenario: Rehearsal feedback notes from the choreographer. Ask them to take turns watching and observing each other performing the selected phrase and to explore giving emphasis to these three things:

Timing: Can they play with the timing? Could it speed up and slow down? Could one action take longer than another?

Dynamics: Can they develop contrasting dynamics? For example, they could explore how to make the faster and smaller actions stand out and the bigger gestures have a sense of weight and flow.

Focus: Ask dancers to bring the phrase to life by exploring where they look or send their eye lines. This includes when they look at the audience, when they look at parts of their bodies and when they look up or down. Where a dancer sends their eye line is also part of the choreography and can layer meaning onto dance actions.

One dancer supports and directs another to refine their dynamics whilst rehearsing.

Teaching Tip

Encourage dancers to make positive observations of their partners and to direct each other in perfecting the action, use of focus, timing and development of contrasting dynamics.

Further Development

Dancers could consider playing the role of choreographer and add or amend whatever they think would make the sequence more interesting to them.

MOMENTS OF STILLNESS

This is a solo task, but it could be explored in pairs, with one being the dancer and the other the choreographer, who suggests actions, makes final decisions and orders movements. Both will need to select a phrase to develop.

1. Ask dancers to recall their own selected phrases and go over them, picking out three positions they can clearly reproduce or are still moments.

2. Encourage them to explore different ways of moving into the first position. They could identify the origin of the energy to perform that movement within the body. They might imagine a pulse of energy creating a pathway through the body until they reach that position.

3. Remind them of their second position and create that shape using the idea of an impulse starting somewhere in the body, perhaps as a reaction to a sound score. They'll need to find a way out of the first position and into the second and consider how slow, small, big, jerky and erratic their movements can be as they send that impulse through the body.

4. Ask the dancers to join all the still moments with this notion of an impulse travelling through different parts of the body. For example, an impulse could happen in a knee, sending energy upwards to the shoulder so that the arm moves into a position. The hand could twitch, sending the energy down the arm and into the shoulder and spine to twist into the next position. You may need to do a simple demonstration if they don't grasp this idea.

5. As they join these, they can allow impulses of movement to flow along different pathways through the body and rehearse it so it looks as seamless, fluid and natural as possible.

6. Ask them to layer two pauses into this phrase. They'll be performing a phrase that uses both pulses and pauses.

Chapter 6 – Developing Improvisations   163

Two dancers perform a phrase together whilst adding in a pause.

Teaching Tip

If dancers picture the energy like a ball that's rolling around inside and being carried from part to part, this will improve the quality of the actions they create.

Further Development

For a challenge, they could find five still moments to work with in step 1 or layer two more into their final phrases.

INTO AND BACK OUT

This development task requires dancers to use the choreographic device referred to as 'additive' or 'incorporative', in which actions are added or incorporated into an existing phrase or sequence. It requires them to consider the level on which actions are performed. It also requires them, in small groups, to create ways to move into, on, along and out of the floor at two points within a given phrase.

1. Ask dancers to form trios and go over their own phrases or sequences, perhaps remembering or beginning to perform it with confidence.

2. Ask the trios to find two moments where the sequence could go into and out of the floor and find an easy way to go down and return.

3. Once they're on the floor, have them find a way to perform the next action that would have been performed at this point on the floor, before returning to standing.

4. Label the dancers A, B and C. The first time they go into the floor, A will remain standing to perform the same actions. The second time, B will remain standing. At the end of the sequence, C can go into the floor and perform one of the moments they missed whilst the others are still.

5. Ask them to select their favourite way into the floor. Once they're at low level, have them create a way to continue travelling on the floor for eight counts. This could be rolling, crawling, turning and spinning, if they keep developing movements they can perform in unison. Ask them to play with adding in a moment of stillness as they travel. They can come out of the floor using the original step up or create their own way at the end of the count.

6. They can combine these two however they choose.

Three dancers learn how going into the floor and being at different levels can create an interesting dance moment.

Teaching Tip

Keeping things simple can often be most effective. Dancers can use each other for ideas and explore them all before selecting final movements.

Further Development

Dancers could extend the floor phrase they've created to last 16 counts.

FORMATION STATION

This task requires groups of four to six dancers to think outside the box and move round the stage space, considering how they use it whilst performing in unison. They'll need to develop a phrase or sequence they already know.

1. Ask them to rehearse the sequence and break it into smaller pieces, numbering each part. This could be as small as three parts or a number for each movement, up to seven.

2. Select the same number of group formations as parts in the sequence. A formation could be a circle, a line, scattered, diagonal lines or a semicircle.

3. Ask dancers to join the movements and formations. They should start dancing in one of these formations, perform their first small part in unison, walk to the next formation and perform their second part.

4. Ask them to decide where they'll face in each formation. For example, will they face the front, side, each other or upstage?

Dancers select a circle formation and face inwards whilst performing their unison phrase.

Teaching Tip

This will be effective if dancers exit and enter each formation from a different direction and perform the movements as soon as they arrive. The walking will work if it's calm but assured.

Further Development

As an additional challenge, dancers could layer in two brief pauses, moments of stillness and a head gesture.

LAYERING IN PATHWAYS

The notion of creating interesting pathways through the dance space forms the basis of this task. Dancers will need an existing phrase or sequence to manipulate.

1. In groups of four or five, ask them to design a floor plan that includes at least three curves and uses the whole stage space. They could write this on paper first, perhaps thinking about how interesting it looks from a design perspective.

2. Ask them to travel in unison in their groups and bring this floor plan to life. Have them add spatial formations to travel in. This could be one formation or they could change (e.g., a diamond to a line or a circle to a square). Ask students to decide how they'll travel whilst performing these floor plans – whether they walk, run, use both or find another way.

3. Ask them to select two to three gestures from their phrase or sequence. They can be from anywhere and not necessarily in any order.

4. Each time dancers change direction, they must perform one of the gestures they've selected. They could also change how they travel (e.g., run, crawl, walk or gallop). Discuss the intention.

Three dancers discuss their pathway designs.

Teaching Tip

Encourage dancers to explore designing interesting floor plans, perhaps by showing ones from other dance works. They could add as many formations as they wish or choose one shape.

Further Development

Students could engage in discussion about what's been created. They could question if the formations they selected are effective and if their pathways demonstrate anything to an audience. They could explore different speeds and layer in facial expressions to add meaning.

ACCUMULATION

This task uses a compositional device called 'accumulation' to create an interesting dance moment. Dancers will need to have an existing phrase or sequence that's known to the whole group.

1. Ask dancers to form groups of five to seven and go over their unison phrase or sequence together.

2. They must divide the sequence into as many parts as there are dancers, plus one more, so each joins in on the sequence one by one. The extra one will be the end, where all the dancers are moving together, so it could be longer than the other parts.

3. Ask them to select a group formation. This could be a pyramid, or they could have one person in front, as a leader, with the others in lines behind.

4. Instruct them to give each other a number (one through six, depending on how many there are), knowing that dancer 1 will begin the actions and may need to be near the front of the formation so they can be seen.

5. Ask dancers to find the starting position, which will be the moment in the phrase or sequence just before they join in. For example, dancer 1 will start at the beginning and dancer 2 will start a few movements in and be almost collected by the group. Before any of them start to move, you'll have a group of dancers, all in different positions and spaces, ready to be picked up within the sequence.

Chapter 6 – Developing Improvisations

A group of dancers are ready to collect each other as they perform an accumulation.

Teaching Tip

Encourage dancers to rehearse this slowly so they can determine how the spacing will work as each joins the phrase or sequence. You might see that one group has understood, or you could talk through the first few moments using one group to demonstrate or decide how the sequence is divided into parts. A mirror will help when rehearsing the accumulations, or you could ask them to stand out and direct the movement and use of space.

Further Development

As a challenge, dancers could reverse the accumulation so they stop, one by one, in a different place or position.

FINDING THE ESSENCE

Often, we, as choreographers, create so much amazing movement material that we can bombard an audience with too much information from the start of a piece. Once we've demonstrated all our best work, where do we go from there? It's better to build ideas from their essence or to have moments that resonate with an audience. Often, these are the more personal, slower, gestural moments in a dance piece. For example, in Crystal Pites' *Flight Pattern*, the movement builds from small head gestures in unison and canon, performed by a large ensemble, into longer, more complex travelling phrases with a full range of body actions. This task will help us understand what resonates with an audience and which movements are more remembered.

1. Ask dancers to form groups of four to five and select a sequence they'd like to explore. They may want to rehearse this in advance.

2. Have them start by standing in a line, one behind the other, with everyone facing in the same direction. Ask them to leave space between each person.

3. Have the dancer at the back of the line start by tapping or saying 'ready' to the one in front. This dancer will turn to face the first, who will perform their sequence whilst being observed. The observer must take in what they see, because they'll have to perform it to the next dancer. Whilst this is happening, the others must wait, facing forwards.

4. Have the second dancer tap or say 'ready' to the next in line. They'll now perform the sequence they were shown to the best of their knowledge, relying on what they remember.

5. The dance will continue down the line until the last dancer, who will teach what they can recall to the original dancer. They can use this sequence or phrase, depending on how short it's become within their dance prior to the sequence they've shared.

6. The groups can start again with a different dancer so all the members can explore how their ideas can be remembered.

A line of dancers discovers where a movement starts and the appropriate quality needed to perform it.

Teaching Tip

This is such an interesting exploration that dancers will want to engage in discussions, so allow for this. It may also have different results with different groups.

Further Development

Dancers could also try this with duets, trios and small group work, but they'd need the movements to be interpreted by the same number of dancers each time it's copied and demonstrated.

REHEARSALS

Most dance companies treat the rehearsal period as an intensely private process and rarely, if ever, let observers in. This task requires dancers to think about the next steps in creating their dance work.

Dancers break down each movement and rehearse to find intention.

1. Ask students to work in pairs and discuss what they think the required skills are for a performer in rehearsal.

2. Ask them to make a list of skills they feel are most important. They might be able to recall, systematically repeat, break down parts, work slowly and mark through and rehearse sections out of order.

3. They can share their observations and thoughts with the rest of the dancers.

4. Instruct them to write a list of rehearsal room or dance studio rules for the company and distribute the list so every member has a copy. They could, perhaps, have a large copy on the rehearsal room wall.

5. Ask them to create a rehearsal plan, considering these questions:

- When and where are you going to meet to rehearse?
- Can you all create a timetable you feel is workable (e.g., everyone can attend, you have space to dance and all the necessary resources are in place)?

Monday	Tuesday	Wednesday	Thursday	Friday

It would make sense if, during rehearsals, dancers do the following:

- Warm up and perform exercises to develop their technical and physical skills.
- Exercise to develop their understanding of style and the themes of their work.
- Rehearse the piece in sections, perhaps dividing up the rehearsal time into solos, duets, trios and so on (dancers could perfect each section once the whole piece is created).
- Engage in individual practice and preparation.
- Perform full run-throughs of the piece, even if it's incomplete.
- Have technical and dress rehearsals.

THE REHEARSAL LOGS

What did you rehearse?
Who did you have to work closely with in this rehearsal and why?
What developments have been made with the piece?
What needs to be developed in the next rehearsal?
Who will you have to contact or liaise with to help meet your group deadlines?
Have you made an action plan for the next rehearsal? What are the main tasks?
How did you apply the principles of safe practice?

COIN CREATIONS

One way to create a structured piece of dance with many collected phrases and sequences as ideas is to use chance. You could create a final piece in this way so the compilation of established movement ideas uses chance but the final piece is set. You could also create a structured improvisation in that you know the movements and music, but the timing and location of the actions in performance could be a split-second decision just before you go on. It could also be something you decide in performance. It's not for everyone, but it can be quite an exciting way to work.

Dancers use a coin to create a chance structure for a known sequence.

1. Resources needed: In pairs, ask dancers to have two sequences each that they've created separately and can easily recall. They may need to take a few minutes to rehearse. They'll need a coin and, perhaps, a pen and paper.

2. There are always two sides to a coin, so ask the pairs to decide which side (heads or tails) belongs to the following:

- Each dancer
- Each of the two sequences
- Alone or complemented by a partner
- Each side of the stage
- A curved or straight pathway

3. Have them throw the coin five times per sequence. This will tell them what will be performed, who will perform it, where it will be performed, what pathway it will use and if it's a solo or duet.

4. Have them throw it another five times and keep going until they've built a possible section of a dance piece. Perhaps they can add a restriction here so they know when it's been completed because it must fit with a chosen piece of music or time frame.

Teaching Tip

If dancers start with short phrases of 4 to 16 counts, they can build a dance quickly.

Further Development

Dancers can add their own rules to the list, like the following:

- Heads: The whole sequence is performed. Tails: Only the first eight counts are performed.
- Heads: The sequence is performed as fast as possible. Tails: The sequence includes moments of stillness.

DISCUSSING DANCE

Sometimes, when dancers are creating a piece of choreography, it can be tricky to gain an overall impression of its message and how it might be received by an audience. Many choreographers refer to this notion of an audience watching for the first time as 'how it lands'. How is your piece landing?

What can a choreographer do to explore how the piece will be viewed or interpreted? It's helpful to be true to your vision, your intention and themes, but if you have all these covered, what else can you do?

Discussing and evaluating improvisations is a useful part of the choreographic process.

Dancers could

- film and watch it back together,
- ask other dancers or choreographers to watch it and give feedback and
- take turns having each group member step out and watch from the audience.

How do you start evaluating the dance piece? Here are a few questions to aid reflection:

1. Does the movement have any meaning or relevance? Is it linked to the dance idea (the stimulus)?

2. What did you want the dance to say or mean?
3. Is the movement material interesting and original in action, dynamics and spatial patterning?
4. Which parts are your favourite? Why?
5. Is there anything you'd like to edit out of the dance?
6. Is there anything you want to add into the dance?
7. Does the movement have the potential for further development?
8. What do you want to do with it next?
9. How will the dance finish?
10. Make a simple plan you can keep to until your next discussion.

CHOREOGRAPHIC TOOL KIT

THE MAIN BODY ACTIONS

Elevation – This is when the whole body moves upwards. It can be rising, lifting or jumping. This term mainly refers to jumping actions, of which there are five:

- Sauté (two feet to two feet)
- Temps levé or hop (one foot to the same foot)
- Jeté, leap or spring (one foot to the other foot)
- Assemblé (one foot to two feet)
- Sissonne (two feet to one foot)

Falling, weight transference or balance – To fall, the body will go through a balance, or transference of weight, first. Falling can be the dropping of a body part or the whole body, where gravity is a factor.

Gesture – This is the movement of one more body parts. It's a non–weight bearing action, usually with an emphasis on expression.

Stillness – This is a pause in the movement when the actions stop for a given amount of time.

Travel – This is a form of physical movement that progresses from one place to another, moving across the general space. The basic locomotor movements include walking, running, skipping, galloping, sliding and leaping.

Turning – This can be rotation of the body parts or, more typically, the whole body, so when a dancer turns, they change where they're facing.

THE DANCE IMPROVISATION AND CHOREOGRAPHIC TOOL KIT

This is a list of terms and choreographic tools that can be applied to and used with the outcomes of the improvisation tasks in this book.

Accumulation

On their own: This refers to building movements by combining them (e.g., movement 1, movement 1 and 2 and so on).

In groups: This is when a dancer performs a series of movements and others join in at different times until all dancers are performing in unison.

Action and Reaction

This is when movements performed by one dancer, or a group of dancers, elicit a response from other dancers.

Additive and Incorporative

This a choreographic device where choreographers add or incorporate new or different movements into a motif or phrase.

Background

This is when any movement is changed but the rest of the body is in its original position, whilst these main actions or gestures are performed.

Canon

This is a movement sequence in which parts are performed in succession, overlapping one another (e.g., reverting, simultaneous and cumulative).

Changing the Use of Dynamics

This is when movements explore varying the energy, intensity, accent and quality.

Communicating Your Dance Intention

This is when the idea, emotion or theme behind a movement or dance piece is explored through the performance or sharing to an audience or peer.

Contact

This occurs when relationships develop between dancers into physical touch. This could include pushing, pulling, nudging, supporting, counterbalancing, lifting and catching.

Contrast

This is used to emphasise differences in dance where movements could differ in energy, use of space, timing, theme or intention.

Counterpoint

This occurs when dancers perform different phrases simultaneously.

Facings and Stage Facings

This is where a dancer faces when performing each action (e.g., downstage, upstage, towards the audience or towards another dancer).

Floor Plan

This is a spatial design that can be seen from above and shows where a dancer has travelled on stage. It's the journey they've taken through general space.

Formations

These are shapes or patterns created in space by dancers.

Fragmentation

This is a choreographic device in which parts of the movements or phrase are split into smaller moments and isolated. They're often reordered or only part of a phrase is used.

Instrumentation

This means to perform a movement with a different body part. For example, an arm circle could become a rond de jambe, or leg circle.

Isolated Movements

These are movements executed with one part or a small area of the body, away from other parts (e.g., rolling the head or shrugging the shoulders).

Levels

This is the distance from the ground (e.g., low, medium or high).

Mirroring

This occurs when movements are performed in unison with dancers facing each other. This means dancers will be using opposite sides of the body.

Musicality

This is a dancer's or a choreographer's attention and responsiveness to musical elements, such as timing, cadence, dynamics or individual instruments.

Narrative Dance

This is a dance that tells a story, often episodic.

Pathways

These are designs traced in space, either on the floor or in the air with body parts.

Planes

There are three planes: horizontal, vertical and sagittal.

Refinement

This is when students hone and perfect a movement or select parts of it that work well.

Repetition

This is performing the same action or phrase again to duplicate it.

Retrograde

This is reversing a movement phrase to reverse the order of a sequence.

Rondo

This is a dance piece in which a section is repeated throughout, like a chorus in a song (e.g., A, B, A, C, A, D and A).

Size

This is simply how big or small a movement is.

Tempo

This is the speed at which a dance or movement is performed.

Transition

This is how one movement, phrase, sequence or section of a dance progresses into the next. It's an idea or movement that links these together.

Unison

This occurs when identical movements are performed at the same time within a group of dancers.

ABOUT THE AUTHOR

Justine Reeve has taught for over 29 years—across all age ranges—and her roles have included teacher, department head, youth dance artistic director, choreographer and consultant.

Ms. Reeve earned her BA (with honours) in dance and related arts and a postgraduate diploma in dance and collaborative arts from the University of Chichester in West Sussex, England, and a postgraduate certificate in education (PGCE). She was the artistic director of the West Sussex Youth Dance Company and a standards verifier for Edexcel/Pearson BTEC levels 2 and 3. She was an A-level dance examiner/moderator for AQA. She is presently an external expert for Ofqual and a moderator for the WJEC exam board.

Stef Kerswell

Ms. Reeve has written units for a well-known exam board's specifications for 10 years and has delivered continued professional development courses for teachers of dance curriculum (key stages 4 and 5) in the United Kingdom for 20 years.

She has written published dance resources for the English National Ballet, Russell Maliphant Dance Company, RSL, Rambert Dance Company, Pearson Education and the London Curriculum for the Mayor of London.

She has been the director of dance at the BRIT School, a dance animateur with Rambert Dance Company and a choreographer with her own company, Puppik Dance. She enjoys visiting the theatre, reading and raising her family.